Reaching the Next Generation For Christ

The Biblical Role of the Family and Church

Dr. Jeff Klick

A Quick Word:

You hold in your hands, or view upon your screen in eBook form, a modified research paper. This work was originally produced to complete part of the requirements for a Ph.D. in pastoral ministry from Trinity Seminary. The pages have been reworked to make them available to a more general readership. My prayer is that this information will be useful to further the discussion of how to reach the next generation for Christ.

Forward

Studies show that multitudes of young people reared in Christian homes are fleeing the Evangelical Church in record numbers as they leave High School. This begs the question as to why. With the emphasis the Church expends, including the huge expense to reach the young, why are we failing?

Is it possible that the Church needs to reevaluate some of what She is doing? Many concerned pollsters state that if changes are not made soon, an entire generation will be lost.

Since the Bible is the Source of all truth, this book will focus on what the Scripture reveals regarding faith impartation to the next generation. In addition, many ancient writers will shed light on what they believed the role of the church and family entailed.

What this book will reveal as it unfolds is, that the Bible is a family centric Book from cover to cover. The specific Biblical commands that exist typically address individuals regarding faith impartation and speak very little to the organized religious community.

While there is room within the realm of preference and necessity for a variety of church models, there is little in the Scripture directly pertaining to their usage.

While many church models are experiencing a huge exodus of young people rejecting their parent's faith as they leave High School, one group in particular stands in startling contrast regarding the ratio of faith adoption. Studies show up to 92% of homeschooled children retaining their parent's faith as they enter college and beyond. The family-integrated church model is primarily populated with home-educated young people, so it is examined in some detail.

The underlying philosophical differences are compared between these two models, primarily focusing on the role of the pastor and the parents, and the evaluation will prove insightful and challenging. The results of this research must not be ignored if we hope to stem the tidal wave of young people rejecting their faith in our generation.

CONTENTS

WITH GRATITUDE!

Thank You Lord Jesus for Your wonderful, saving grace! Thank you Leslie for being my dearest companion for all these years. Thank you Andrea, Sarah and David, my arrows that are making a difference in this world. Also, thank you for all those wonderful grandchildren - Lydia, Katelyn, Mackenzie, Daniel, Nathan, Havilah, Adrielle, Gabriel, Alexis, and Treya, Thank you to the wonderful folks at Hope Family Fellowship that love the Lord, their families, and each other. What a blessing!

1 THE PROBLEM WE FACE

It is hard to forget the picture that popped up on the computer screen one morning while perusing some typical news outlets. Two pre-teens were dangling their younger sibling out of a window in a high-rise apartment building by his hands. The two in the window stood expressionless in the photo shortly before letting the child drop multiple stories to his death. Moreover, how could anyone forget the tragedy of the Columbine massacre, the mall killings in Minnesota by yet another gun-wielding student, or the recent school shooting in Sandy Hook Connecticut? By just about any standard used, the young people in America are in serious trouble, and have been since the late 1950's.

We are bombarded daily with statistics giving us far too many details including: teen crime rates, teen pregnancy and abortion, the impact of divorce, drug and alcohol abuse (even in pre-high school age children), suicide, and unthinkable violence, each of which are taking an incredible toll on the next generation.

Since 1991, the United States government has been conducting anonymous surveys specifically attempting to categorize the risky behaviors of youth. While the statistics are interesting, it will not do to bore the reader with the plethora of dangerous and sometimes deadly behavior engaged in by our young people.

The title of the study, – *Morbidity and Mortality Weekly Report,*[1] and the necessity of having to keep track of such things for our school age children is disturbing enough to illustrate that there are substantial problems in our culture.

In 1993, William Bennett shared a staggering statistic: "Violent crimes have increased 400 percent since 1960, with the most active incubator of this violence centered in the 10 to 17 year old age group."[2] Of course, many have come to expect that from non-Christian, unchurched young people, but this must surely be different in the Evangelical Church.

The organized church spends tens of millions of dollars each year to reach Christian youths via youth ministry and Christian schools.[3] A quick Google search will reveal hundreds, if not thousands of Christian youth organizations worldwide. A partial listing includes the following: Youth for Christ, Youth Specialties, Youth Unlimited, Youth Ministry Exchange, Legacy Youth Ministries, National Youth Ministries, Teen Life Ministries, ELCA Youth Ministries, GBOD Youth Ministries, PCUSA Youth Ministries, Teen Missions, AFLC Youth Ministries, Nazarene Youth Ministries, etc. This list does not include Christian school ministries or curriculum producers

---

[1]. United States Government, "Morbidity and Mortality Weekly Report," June 6, 2008, Surveillance Summaries, http://www.cdc.gov/mmwr (accessed August 5, 2008).

[2]. William J. Bennett, *The Index of Leading Cultural Indicators* (Washington, DC: The Heritage Foundation, 1993), 13.

[3]. Syndicate PayScale Data, "Salary Survey Report for Job: Youth Pastor," 9/4/2008, http://www.payscale.com/research/US/Job=Youth_Pastor (accessed September 13, 2008). This survey for example, only represents less than 100 youth ministers and is already in excess of 2 million dollars, and does not include anything spent on annual budgets. Tens of millions is probably a very low estimate of the annual expenditure for youth ministry.

exclusively devoted to reaching the young. In addition, just about all major denominations are deeply involved in youth and children's ministry in some fashion. With such massive expenditures of time, money, and staff devoted to reaching young people, the Evangelical Church should be *excelling* in their goal of reaching the next generation for Christ.

However, consider some of these disturbing statistics: George Barna, a well-known pollster that focuses primarily on the Christian marketplace, recently released a study showing that only twenty percent of teenagers retain their faith after they reach adulthood.[4] A twenty percent success rate translates into *four out of five* youths leaving their faith shortly after graduating from high school. In addition, Mr. Barna maintains that if current trends continue, in ten years, church attendance will be half the size it is today.[5]

Dawson MacAlister, national youth ministry specialist, remarked that 90% of youth active in high school church programs drop out of church by the time they are sophomores in college.[6] Southern Baptists, known for devoting large sums of time and money to Sunday school programs and youth outreach, also are struggling. At a recent Southern Baptist Convention, data presented indicated that 70-88% of their youth left after their first year in college.[7] In the same study, the Southern Baptist Council on Family Life reported an even more staggering statistic: 88% of children in evangelical homes leave church at

---

[4]George Barna, "Most Twentysomethings Put Christianity on the Shelf Following Spiritually Active Teen Years," September 11, 2006, http://www.barna.org (accessed April 8, 2008).

[5]George Barna, *Revolution* (Carol Stream, Illinois: Tyndale House Publishers, 2005), 48.

[6]Reggie McNeal, *The Present Future* (San Francisco, California: Bass, Jossey, 2003), 4.

[7]T. C. Pinkney, *Remarks to the Southern Baptist Convention Executive Committee* (Nashville, Tennessee, 2001). September 18, 2001.

the age of eighteen.

Scott Brown, the director of The National Center for Family Integrated Churches reveals some insightful statistics from Thomas Rainer. Dr. Rainer formerly served as a professor of evangelism at Southern Baptist Seminary. His survey was concerned with people's general understanding of the Gospel and the application to their personal life beyond the walls of the Church:

> Born before 1946 — 65%, Born between 1946 and 1964 — 35%, Born between 1965 and 1976 — 15%, Born between 1976 and 1994 — 4%.[8]

The comprehension of the Gospel, and what it means to live like a Christian, based on this survey, seems to be in a free fall from the 1940's to the 1990's. A drop of 61% between 1946 and 1994 is staggering.

A four-year study conducted by Professors Webber, Dr. Mason, Dr. Singleton, and Rev. Dr. Hughes, demonstrated this current deficiency in reaching youths. The parents of the students sent their children to a Christian school, at least partially for spiritual reasons, yet the students considered the intrusion of the staff and administration as a violation of their freedom.

> They objected to the school that taught them what they should believe. "Our principal pretty much told us we had to believe in God and the Church," said one student attending a Christian school. "Kind of annoying because we all feel that we want to believe in what we want to," she continued. "I was kind of confused. I just thought we

---

[8]. Scott Brown, "The Greatest Untapped Evangelistic Opportunity Before The Modern Church," Vision Forum, http://www.visionforumministries.org/issues (accessed May 6, 2008).

don't have to do that because you tell us to." Their parents often have similar attitudes and are no more involved in the churches than their children.[9]

Based on this sampling of studies referenced, it should be clear that the next generation of the Church is struggling to follow in the previous one's footsteps, or considering the last quote, perhaps not. Parents have a tremendous amount of influence over their children's behavior, and ultimately whether their children accept or reject Christianity. However, it is possible they do not understand what they wield. It should be readily apparent that the parents and the church are both struggling to capture the next generation for Christ, in spite of the significant cost and the time exerted.

Surveys and studies are not completely reflective of reality though: many ministries are exceeding the previously quoted statistics. In addition, not all churches are experiencing these disappointing results. Nonetheless, these studies *do* reflect a reality that many groups are facing, and are therefore representative of an issue worth studying. The many groups that are experiencing these trends realize that if even the smaller percentage of 70% were used instead of the 90%, it would still be considered a miserable failure by any objective standard. The statistics raise the question as to *why* this is happening. The purpose of this book is to analyze where the problem in the failure to impart the parents' belief system to a significant percentage of churched youth may rest, and to determine if there are any guidelines available within the Scripture that suggest a remedy.

---

[9]Christian Research Association, "Implication of the Study of Youth Spirituality," September, 2006, http://www.cra.org.au/pages/000000269.cgi (accessed April 11, 2008).

The Evangelical Church appears to understand the dilemma to some degree, and is seeking answers through prayer. With the advent of the Internet, we can perform easy searches and discover such headlines as these: "Methodist Youth Conference Calls for Prayer for Revival,"[10] "Sparking Revival in Tomorrow's Church Leaders,"[11] "Pray for Revival in Youth Ministries,"[12] and, finally, "The Call,"[13] which is a national group dedicated to praying specifically for revival among the Christian youth. These websites calling for prayer point out that there is a cry for revival directed towards the youth from many within the Evangelical Church. Revival is typically defined as "an act or instance of reviving: the state of being revived."[14]

For something to be revived there must have been something lost or diminished. What has been lost is the faith and observable Christian behavior that is supposed to be passed on from parent to child. According to the data quoted above, the Church and Christian parents are failing in large numbers to instill their belief system into the next generation. The churches, schools, and youth ministries understand the need and that is why they pray for revival. Frustrated with their lack of success they call out to God to stir up the hearts of their youth.

---

[10]Christian Today, "Methodist Youth Conference Calls for Prayer of Revival," Wednesday, June 28, 2006, Christian Today, http://www.christiantoday.com/article/myc.call.for.prayer.for.re vival/6763.htm (accessed April 11, 2008).

[11]"Sparking Revival in Tomorrow's Church Leaders," April 9, 2008, http://www.gospel.com (accessed April 11, 2008).

[12]"Pray 4 Revival Youth Ministries," N/A, http://www.injesus.com (accessed April 11, 2008).

[13]"The Call DC," April 11, 2008, http://www.thecall.com (accessed April 11, 2008).

[14]In *Merriam-Webster*, http://www.merriam-webster.com/dictionary/revival (accessed April 11, 2008).

Personal Experience

While serving in a variety of ministerial positions for over three decades, my experiences have raised a desire to understand why there is such a significant failure ratio in passing the faith on to the next generation. I served in a number of relevant functions; youth pastor, an associate pastor, an administrative pastor over a large Christian school, and a senior pastor. In addition, I have been married more than thirty-eight years, and have raised three adult children, who have all retained their faith. We currently have ten grandchildren that are walking in the footsteps of their parents and grandparents. This life experience also provides numerous insights into the problem of failing to pass on the faith.

Reluctantly serving as a youth pastor, I interacted with hundreds of young people every week, and participated in many citywide outreach efforts that were combined with other youth ministries in the city. While some of this effort was geared to the unchurched, the vast majority of the sizable church's budget and time was invested in attempting to reach the children of those already *in* the church. The youth pastors in Kansas City offered much prayer in seeking revival in the churched youth. The highlight of any given year came during the annual combined summer camp, with hundreds of churched youths in attendance. Here, the leaders could always expect a major response to the evening altar call during the Wednesday evening message. Many would come forward and confess Christ. The youth pastors were amazed to count the number of young people that had grown up in a Christian home, attend a Christian school, faithfully participated in weekly youth meetings, and yet, did not know Jesus Christ as savior.

While serving as the pastor and elder in charge of the Christian school, I was able to interact one-on-one with more than sixty Christian high school students in their junior and senior years. Only a few students were clearly excited to be living as Christians. These few students timidly confided to me that they were often the victims of harassment from other students and even from some faculty, which they suffered because of their spiritual zeal.

The church sponsoring this Christian school spent over $330,000 per year on this ministry.[15] While its academic achievements were impressive, the spiritual development was severely lacking, and was not sufficient enough to exceed the failure ratio mentioned above. The school administrator stated, "That it really didn't matter if kids went to private or public school, what mattered ultimately was how much the parents were involved. The parental involvement would help determine how successful the transition of the belief system would end up being in the life of the student."

In addition to serving as a youth pastor, I also participated in Bible Quizzing, which provided a significant amount of contact with hundreds of children, ages eleven through nineteen, in a very competitive environment. In Kansas City, there is a very active group with dozens of teams from multiple denominations. In addition, there are regional events, as well as the large, national tournament that is attended by thousands of youths from all over United States. Coaching teams both locally and nationally provided me with another point of contact with young people from many denominational backgrounds. Similar to the citywide annual youth summer camps previously mentioned, the National Bible Quizzing Tournament[16] would always give an

[15]. Association of Christian Schools International, "2007 ACSI Annual Report," 2007, http://www.acsi.org/webfiles/webitems/attachments/002991_2 007 Annual Report.pdf (accessed September 13, 2008). ACSI represents 5,500 schools worldwide and boast a budget of over 20 million dollars of assets.

[16]. Bible Quizzing Fellowship, "Bible Quiz Fellowship - A

opening rally altar call. Again, many young people would go forward to receive Christ as their savior. Most of these young people had spent months memorizing large quantities of Scripture, and yet they did not know the Author of them.

While I was serving as the executive pastor of a large church, the senior pastor desired to make a philosophical change in the youth ministry that involved a radical decision. Being keenly aware of the difficulties of youth ministry, when I was approached by the senior pastor to take over the program, "shocked" is not too strong of a word to explain everyone's reaction. Since I had no experience in youth work, a decision was made to invest in an educational trip to a national youth workers convention in Atlanta.[17]

A few eager youth workers, in addition to me, entered into a mostly empty and cavernous auditorium. Fifteen minutes after the scheduled time to begin, a rather scraggly-looking man with a guitar sauntered on to the stage with a stool in hand. By this time, a few others, looking very similar to the man on stage, had plopped down into the seats in the auditorium. The man with the guitar sat down and began to play "Sitting on the Dock of the Bay" and some felt that he must have been in the wrong place. Somehow, the youth workers must have missed the youth training meeting and ended up in a reunion of old hippies.

For the remainder of the conference, I made every effort to be open-minded, and dutifully continued attending the workshops. Over 1,000 leaders in attendance learned how to sneak into a teenager's room and video tape them while they slept. The men and women learned how to make peanut butter and jelly sandwiches under their armpits to gross out the teens. In addition, instruction was given as to how to play group games,

---

Fellowship of Youth Ministries," http://www.biblequizfellowship.org (accessed September 13, 2008).

[17]. National Youth Workers Convention, http://www.nywc.com.

role playing games, party games, organize social outings, get a bigger budget, and a host of other intriguing ideas, but very little about how to train young people to mature and to follow Christ. During one of the group gatherings the leader on the platform asked, "How many of you need a revival in your youth group?" Almost every hand enthusiastically shot up, thus confirming the previous observations made in the earlier section of this book.

In order to fully flesh out my experiences, we must leave the United States. Having the opportunity to travel to Mexico, the Philippines, and China provided me a larger view of Christian youth than is available in the United States. In observing and interacting with the Christian youth of these countries, one will typically find that much of what American youths take for granted is non-existent in these other places. In Mexico, I spent a week building basic housing for hurricane-ravaged victims, and found that, the teens were mostly concerned about the survival of their families, and had very little time for the issues that consume so many American teens. Name brand clothing or expensive shoes were immaterial. Outside appearances such as hairstyle or jewelry mattered little. Age-segregation was unheard of, for everyone was in the same plight, living in a one-room house.

In the Philippines, the living conditions were even worse. A four-block area called "the killing fields" gave shelter to tens of thousands of people. The daily struggle for food, clean water, and shelter absorbed most of young people's time.

In multiple visits to China, staying in a university town, these struggles for the daily necessities were not so prevalent. The students were very serious about their studies, and most acknowledged free time as a gift, not a birthright. Diligence and respect demonstrated toward adults were normal behaviors, not the whining and self-focus that so many American teens demonstrate. The Christian young people in all three nations were exceptional in their behavior and in their diligence, and very little of the typical trappings of the American youth were evident. It makes one wonder if the difficult life styles that they grew up in helped them so much more than the affluence of the typical American teen. This thought is however, beyond the nature of this book.

The experience received while serving in the ministry at a hyper-growth, large church is another factor that shapes the desire to write this book. Being hired as the first church administrator at age twenty-four provided many opportunities to view church-growth first hand. The church, at this time, had 1,100 people in attendance in the Sunday services, yet had only three full-time pastors. There were few designations or departments at this stage of the church's development. As more people attended, and the cash flowed in freely, additional staff was added, as well as the departmental model. First, a music minister was hired. Next, a children's pastor, youth pastor, singles' pastor, home group pastor, counseling pastor, missions' pastor, full-time sound person, and a nursery coordinator. Of course, the necessary support staff was added as needed. The church continued to add new members weekly, and the financial resources were abundant.

The Christian school was also growing annually at an astounding rate. Soon a second tier of K through 12 classes was added to meet the increasing demand. From all outside appearances the ministry was very successful having more than 3,500 in attendance on Sundays, and over 600 students in the school. The staff swelled to over 100 employees between the church and school. The network of churches associated with this large church in the city expanded to more than forty. In spite of the external success, the results with young people in all of the churches were in line with the studies referenced in chapter one. Large sums of money were spent in targeted ministry, and tremendous human resources were added to reach the young people for Christ, yet the results were in line with aforementioned studies.

The church provided care for the children in nurseries, trained them in Sunday school and children's church, had a dynamic youth ministry, enrolled them in Christian school, and ended up praying for their salvation and revival as they left in droves. These young people should have been stellar examples of an effective ministry and instead they were leaving the faith and church in huge numbers.   Something was amiss. John Angell James (1785-1859) stated the dilemma well,

> The best possible scheme of Christian education, most judiciously directed and most perseveringly maintained, has in some cases totally failed.[18]

A Roadmap

The current age-segregated model used by many Evangelical Churches will be examined in chapter two and, in addition, a brief historical sketch on how and when this philosophy developed will be presented. The Scripture will serve as the primary source for the study and conclusions, so an in-depth analysis of the applicable verses, with relevant comments by Biblical scholars, will follow in subsequent chapters. In this presentation of Scripture, some of the main Biblical characters will be examined, specifically in light of their parenting, with an emphasis on their successes and failures.

A pattern will emerge that demonstrates the parents are primary responsibility for the impartation of faith into the next generation and not the organized religious community. In addition, the role of each family member will be discussed, dealing specifically with his or her individual responsibilities as

---

[18]. John Angell James, "Principle Obstacles in Bringing Up Children for Christ," *Free Grace Broadcaster* 208 (Summer 2008), 34.

revealed by the research. The Scripture will then be examined to determine what role the Church should be exercising in the impartation of faith to the next generation.

2 THE AGE-SEGREGATED CHURCH MODEL

To begin this section, two prejudices must be acknowledged before presenting the information covered in this chapter. Before becoming a Christian on July 25, 1973, I was firmly engaged in the drug culture. My life consisted of loud rock and roll, illicit sex, drugs and alcohol, and a generally rebellious lifestyle in thought and deed. The memory of such a lifestyle is still fresh and can possibly influence my objectivity. When similar activities are encountered today in the Christian arena, it is reminiscent of what was experienced before being gloriously delivered by salvation. 3 John 11 states, "Beloved, do not imitate evil but imitate good."

When the Christian community shows any imitation of the world's practices, it is hard to remain objective. In addition, as shared in the previous chapter, I spent years working in and around youth ministry interacting with hundreds of young people, and so it is impossible not to be influenced by these personal experiences, both good and bad, in any analysis of Biblical truth. In some ways, everyone is tempted to approach the Scripture expecting to find what they are looking for, and not necessarily, what is actually there, and I am not immune.

As mentioned previously, current trends show a significant rejection of the Christian faith in young people upon graduation of high school. Many of these young people have been reared in the age-segregated model of ministry presented in the Church and Christian school. What follows are personal observations from decades of interacting with youth ministries in multiple states around the USA, and readily available information from published literature and websites by some of the youth ministries referred to in chapter one. I have personally attended some of this training and have led hundreds of local, as well as many national youth events, in a variety of denominational formats.

The following descriptions of events and gatherings are presented as being "typical."[19] By using the word "typical," it is intended to mean, "being representative of," and not meaning to reflect what takes place in *every* youth group or *every* church. It is necessary to have at least some understanding of what is experienced in the "typical" Evangelical church in order to make an effective comparison to the Scripture in subsequent chapters. For the sake of simplicity, the word, "typical" will not be referenced from this point on, but let the reader understand that is what is meant.

If you visit an Evangelical church youth group or event, you will most likely find loud, modern music as well as many couples engaging in plenty of public displays of affection. The group or meeting will be led by a person that is slightly older than the attendees are, but not so much older that they are perceived to be from a different generation. Many youth gatherings provide a "mixer" of some sort to begin the meeting. This activity is intended to break the ice and encourage communication between the teens. These activities often include such tasks as passing a piece of candy from toothpick to toothpick between mouths (with both genders involved) without dropping it. Another

[19]. Ministry.com, "YouthMinistry.com - One Place, Infinite Ideas," http://www.youthministry.com (accessed September 13, 2008). This site would be representative of what the researcher means by "typical."

popular activity is the placing of a balloon between a girl and boy, and making sure it stays there by firmly embracing each other front to front, as they walk across the room. Icebreaker games come in all sizes and fashions, and while there is no reason to oppose having fun, one has to wonder about the results of encouraging hormonally charged teenagers to touch each other in such ways. (Perhaps a subsequent study should delve into this thought.)

Some of the games are harmless and others border on the obscene. For example, a particular website for icebreaker type games is entitled "Sick and Twisted Games."[20] Not all of the games listed on the website are demented or bizarre, but several certainly do match the title. For example, "Bobbing for Worms," "Condiment Twister," and "Cricket Spit." Young men and women being tangled together on a plastic mat covered in ketchup and mustard will most likely produce an abundance of laughter, but probably not promote moral chastity. Another popular activity, personally witnessed at a nationally youth leadership seminar, involves a youth leader removing his shirt and applying peanut butter under his right armpit, and jelly under the left one. Afterwards, bread was given to him to rub off the materials, and then a challenge was given for someone to eat it.

Consider another one that certainly ranks high on the disgusting meter:

> A youth leader chewed up a mixture of dog food, sardines, potted meat, sauerkraut, cottage cheese, and salsa, topped off with holiday eggnog….he then spit out the mixture into a glass and encouraged the members of the youth group to drink it. Finally, there is a game where the youth director asks the young people to line up. Each person

[20]. The Source for Youth Ministry, "Sick and Twisted Games," http://www.thesource4ym.com/games/sick.asp (accessed July 10, 2008).

brushes his teeth with the same toothbrush and spits into the same cup and the last person in line drinks what is in the cup.[21]

All of the activities seem to have a two-fold purpose. First, the breaking down of social barriers that may exist between male and female, and, second, letting young people understand that the leader is really a fun-loving person. The rapport between the youth leader and the group seems to be important to helping facilitate the transference of the youth leader's vision to the group.

After some sort of icebreaker, "worship" often follows. Usually led by teens, this experience can range from moving to painful. The music presented will typically include someone playing a guitar, a keyboard, drums, and the bass. The bass player will most likely have some sort of soft drink that has to be placed on the over-sized speaker that is capable of filling a room ten times the size it currently dwarfs. If the group of musicians is proficient, the worship can be moving and uplifting. If the group is less than spiritual, the worship can be distracting and self-exalting.

One observation that has been made over the years is how teens worship in the "adult" church as compared to in their youth group. Many times, it seems that the teen can hardly stand up and must lean on the back of the seat or pew in front of them to keep from falling down during the main worship service. On the other hand, this docile individual may be very exuberant in the smaller group, and one has to wonder, "why?" Is it that, unless the beat of the music is pounding in the chest, worship cannot be enjoyed, or is it peer pressure? Having the opportunity to ask many young people this question, the response received is usually, "I'm tired." It makes one wonder what they were doing

---

[21]J. Mark Fox, *Family Integrated Church* (Camirillo, California: Salem Communications, 2006).

on Saturday night, but that is outside the scope of this book.

If there is a sermon given at the gathering it will be primarily focused towards the world in which the youth live. Titles such as, "How to Get over a Break Up with Your Significant Other," or "Is There Truth in Your X File?"[22] are presented in order to be relevant. There may or may not be any Scripture used, and if a Bible story is told, there most likely will not be much theology or doctrine covered, because the material presented must be relevant, not boring. One constant trend among youth leaders is to often plunge down to where the young people are mentally, behaviorally, emotionally and spiritually. Most young people state that they want to be treated as adults, yet by observing a typical youth worker it seems that the workers are consistently attempting to dress and act exactly like a teen, so they can be relevant and accepted.

The youth group may spend time in other "spiritual" activities, but for the most part whatever is done needs to be fast paced, and to change often. Youth leaders are told that the youth needs activities, social interaction, constant change, and almost continuous movement. There is a reason that most youth leaders are barely out of their teens, older men cannot keep up the pace! It would seem perfectly normal that many teens are bored with "adult church" after spending their initial church life in the fast paced, entertainment oriented, boy-girl focused gatherings. It seems that it would hard for the youth to find anything of interest in prayer, hymns, and doctrine-laced sermons.

The pattern of ministry described above is also followed in children's church, junior church, pre-teen church, and some other alternatives to the service attended by the adults. The separation of the family begins shortly after a child is born and the church encourages the parent to place the baby in the loving

---

[22]. Ministry.com, "YouthMinistry.com - One Place, Infinite Ideas," http://www.youthministry.com (accessed September 13, 2008).

care of a nursery worker. Toddlers are moved to another nursery, and entertained with crackers, juice, soda, and stories. Older toddlers are told Bible stories by huge dogs or puppets, and when a child reaches the age of twelve, they are placed in "adult church." Ask almost any young person trained in this atmosphere about "adult church" and the response you will most likely receive is, "It's boring!" Since birth, the child has been held, coddled, fed, entertained, and dazzled. They have laughed, colored, made paper angels, and watched fast-paced videos and puppets for years, then suddenly they are told to enter the worship service of the adults, and many wonder why they find it boring. Some churches decide that they need to speed up their own services to make sure the young people in attendance are happy. Alternatively, they add a children's segment of some sort, or drama, or video, or loud music. Why? Because 70 to 90% [23]of the young people leave the church, when they reach adulthood and something must be done.

The Evangelical Church did not always function under the concept of age-segregated ministry. The segregating of the children and youth away from adults, thus providing their own age oriented service, has, when viewed historically, only recently become the normal way of training. While there have been efforts made to make the Bible relevant to the various ages through classes, the normal pattern was for the family to be intact during the primary worship service.

How Did We Get Here?

This book is not intended to digress into a detailed history lesson, so it will briefly touch on some of the major events that lead to the place where we currently find the state of thought in

[23]. Barna, Most Twentysomethings Put Christianity on the Shelf Following Spiritually Active Teen Years," http://www.barno.org.

church age-segregated ministry. Many of these points are common knowledge, so, for the sake of brevity, they will not be thoroughly developed. Before the industrial revolution, it was almost impossible, and probably unthinkable, to divide the family. The majority of families provided their own food, clothing, and basic needs. For thousands of years the vast majority of young men and women followed in their parents' footsteps without any hesitation, because so few other options were available concerning a different career path.

During and after the "revolution," many men moved to the city where work was plentiful, and where the family unit would never be the same. As education began to be considered more important, the one-room schoolhouse was often the normal experience. Within this classroom would sit all levels of ages and learning abilities, and it did not seem to matter how old someone was, for the students were educated at their current level without regard to age segregation. In the same classroom would sit an eight year old and a fifteen year old, and it was considered normal.

In the reading of history books, it would be hard to find a "generation gap" before the 1950's and it must be asked as to why it exists now. While it is difficult to pinpoint the exact time the societal understanding moved from children being simply young adults to its own separate class of individuals, the following quotes shed some insight into the process and perhaps some unintended consequences of the decisions that were made.

> Age was not even included as a category in the 1850 census, it was not considered important. Even in social gatherings, children, who were considered to be miniature adults, mingled with people much older than themselves.[24]

---

[24]Chris Schlect, "A Critique of Youth Ministries," http://www.soulcare.org/education/youth (accessed April 12, 2008).

In prior generations, children were not isolated into separate groups away from the adults but were included in the same social circle. While they may have been required to be quiet in the presence of adults, they were still expected to learn something from being in their proximity. Of course, they would be treated and perhaps educated differently from adults at times, but not segregated or allowed to function as a separate group of people, as is common in our day.

> In 1904, G. Stanley Hall's multivolume tome, *Adolescence* was published. He claimed that a period of crisis came at adolescence, which he considered the most critical period in one's life. This time in life was seen to be so important that it separated teens from those older and younger to them. In short, G. Stanley Hall invented adolescence.[25]

Hall suggested in this groundbreaking book, that individuals roughly evolve through the same stages which human history has evolved. A critical transition period led to the adolescent years of 8 to 12, which were likened to the early pygmies and other savages, followed by the teen years which were an all together different sort of animal. Whether Mr. Hall actually did invent adolescence or not, the view taken in his book certainly did change the way children and teens were viewed.

Charles Silberman credits Boston, Massachusetts, as the first city to have a school where students studied year round, and where instructors had fifty-five students each:

> The fact is that most American schools were ungraded until the second half of the nineteenth century, the graded school having been introduced in the United States in 1848, when the Quincy Grammar School in Boston,

---

[25]Ibid.

Massachusetts, opened its doors.. [26]

The men, who created the graded school concept, predicted that it would set the pattern of American schooling for another fifty years. They obviously underestimated their impact and longevity.

Age segregation is now the norm, and is constantly being refined. In the 1950's there were few junior high or middle schools, though both exist today in large numbers. The underlying philosophy for this invention is commonly understood that the older children need to be separate so that the negative influences can be limited. Thus, today there is high school, middle school, elementary school, and preschool to ensure that there is little contact between the age groups. Many in the Evangelical Church have adopted this same pattern of segregation for religious education via Sunday school programs and Christian schools. By isolating the age groups, it seems that a great deal of wisdom and experience is lost. However, given our current state of affairs, it is probably safer to adopt this viewpoint so that younger children will not be corrupted as quickly by premature contact with the older ones.

New social groups were formed as a consequence of the age-isolation process, but as the Alban Institute states, these might have been the result of something better lost:

> In the past century, contacts across age groups were naturally fostered in tightly knit and age-layered communities. Lacking such community-grounded contacts now, people find their social networks among those of their own age group.[27]

---

[26]. John Silberman, *Crisis in The Classroom: The Remaking of American Education* (New York, NY: Random House, 1970), 166.
[27]. Healy, Anthony E, "Questioning the Age-Segregated Church," September, 2003,

The transference and even cross-pollination of wisdom, character, and culturally accepted norms, appears to be struggling in our day. The gap between the age groups has produced ample marketing opportunities for savvy businesses, but little sharing of values. A daily dose of horrors via TV or news outlets will likely readily confirm the loss of values. Little respect is shown for the aged, the infirmed, the unborn, and those that are less fortunate. Without the wisdom of the older to guide the younger, values will continue to slide downward towards self-centeredness.

One day I asked a Christian school administrator the following questions: "Why does the Christian school exactly imitate the methods of salary structure and classroom breakdown by age that the public system uses, since Christian schools were formed due to being diametrically opposite?" In addition, the administrator was also asked. "Why do you financially reward those with more education in the system that you oppose, for example, someone with a Master's degree gets paid higher than a BA, yet Christian education was created as a result of being against the public system in which they received the education?

His answer ("because everyone else does it that way,") did not provide a satisfactory response to the posed questions. This conversation is included to point out how easy it is to adopt a system without ever considering its roots, or what it is imitating. The issue was not salaries, but the method for determining them. The incremental adoption of an unbiblical system in Christianity can lead to serious problems without its users ever being aware of the process that initiated it.   The Church has, on occasions throughout history, adopted the secular world's systems, and has invariable suffered for it. For example, centuries after the joining of the civil and religious branches of Rome, a Reformation was required to separate them, suggesting that they probably should

http://www.alban.org/conversation.aspx?id=2416 (accessed September 19, 2008).

not have been co-mingled. The Church needs to evaluate *why* they do things, not only what they are doing.

By the 1950's, teens had their own music, literature, styles of dress, language, and etiquette. Generational differences hitherto unheard of became obvious and accepted. Thus was born the generation gap that was uncommon in previous generations. What has transpired since this gap was invented is disastrous. The rebellion of the 60's and 70's unleashed abortion on demand, drug and alcohol usage of unimaginable proportions, "free sex," rampant divorce, and rebellion as normal and accepted behaviors. The high school years often become idolized as the greatest, most important part of someone's life. By the time someone reaches age thirty, they are now considered over the hill, and many end up having mid-life crises attempting to deal with their fleeting youth. An anonymous quote has correctly stated, "unless this pattern changes, we have doomed our society to the pursuit of perpetual immaturity."

Around the 1950's, a new outreach phenomenon appeared entitled "parachurch ministries." Groups entitled, "Youth for Christ," "Campus Crusade for Christ," and others specifically targeted reaching the youth as a subculture. As these groups swelled in numbers, the local churches apparently took notice and began to rethink age integration and their ministry approach. Historically the senior pastor taught everyone, and the parents were responsible for making sure that the children gleaned what they could from the messages as the sermon was discussed over the afternoon meal. In order to compete with these growing youth oriented meetings, churches began to hire youth ministers and specifically target this newly created demographic.

During the 70's, 80's, and continuing through today, the Evangelical church had segregated to such an extent that, in many churches there are multiple weekly meetings, and staff required for every age between birth and twenty-five year olds. These staff positions often included- Children's Church, Junior

Church, Youth Church, Senior High Church, Young Singles, College and Career, Older Singles, Young Married, Young Married with Kids, and Young Married without Kids. In addition, churches routinely offer classes for every school-age group and for those married based on age, as well as classes and events geared to the "senior saints."

The Typical Understanding of Family Ministry

Many churches include the term "family" in their name or literature, and what is understood is separation, not the integration of family.[28] "We are a family-oriented church" or "A place where the whole family is loved" will scroll across a typical church website. What is meant is that every member of the family has a place to be divided to from birth to nursing home age. The age-segregation process is practiced and accepted as normal, being now the standard method of operation in the vast majority of Evangelical churches.

This process is so well engrained that many young pastors look forward to the day when they can hire their first staff person- typically a children's or youth pastor. In 1993, there was a monthly meeting with seven or eight other pastors in the Western part of Shawnee, Kansas. These men were all beginning new church works, so they gathered, sharing their visions, and praying together for mutual support. The meeting would rotate between each pastor's meeting place or office. One day, the meeting was held in the rented offices of one of the men that truly grasped the current age-segregated vision. This man had around thirty people in his congregation yet rented enough office space for a large staff and employed a full-time secretary. As he

[28]. First Family Church, "Welcome to First Family Church," October, 2008, First Family Church, http://www.ffc.org (accessed October 2, 2008). This church in Kansas City has 81 ministries for every member of the family from cradle to grave.

walked through the hall, he would point out the signs that were on each door; "future youth minister," "future children's pastor," "future Sunday school coordinator" "future single's minister" etc. The vision for an age-segregated church was in full display and it is the generally accepted pattern for achieving success. Success is often defined as a large congregation, abundant budget, and growing staff to lead a department oriented ministry.

Next Stop:

In chapters three and four, we will begin to delve into the Scriptures in search of finding patterns regarding faith impartation to the next generation. Chapter three will develop the Old Testament and chapter four the New.

3 THE VIEW FROM THE OLD TESTAMENT

The *Westminster Confession of Faith* was published in 1647 and contains the following statement residing under point #6:

> The whole counsel of God concerning all things necessary for his own glory, man's salvation, faith and life, is either expressly set down in Scripture, or by good and necessary consequence may be deduced from Scripture: unto which nothing at any time is to be added, whether by new revelations of the Spirit, or traditions of men.[29]

While some may disagree with the totality of the views of the Confession, many evangelicals would be fairly comfortable with the above quotation, believing that the Scripture is the standard to be adhered to for faith and practice. Traditional evangelicals believe that the Scripture is God's revelation of Himself, His will for His people, and the unveiling of His eternal plan. The understanding of the primacy of Scripture underpins this book about what has been revealed in God's Word specifically concerning the family and the Church, and their respective roles in faith transference to the next generation.

---

[29]Orthodox Presbyterian Church, "Westminster Confession of Faith," http://www.opc.org/wcf.html (accessed April 15, 2008).

As the Scriptural texts are examined, observable patterns and principles regarding the family will become clearer as well as what role the Church, and pre-church, ordered religious systems played, in passing faith on to the next generation. Another important point of this examination of the Scripture is to determine if *any* pattern or practice that reinforces the age-segregation model commonly practiced today emerges. This chapter will primarily look at the Old Testament and the next chapter will delve into the New.

Before examining specific texts, one has to reflect on the underlying concept of the family in a general sense. Consideration should be given as to *why* God chose this structure to introduce humans to the world, instead of some other viable group. Fish have schools and animals have packs, so why are humans birthed into a family structure? God could have had humans created from rocks, or simply have them hang like ripe fruit from a "human tree" like an orange. Biblical and theological understanding allows us a glimpse into what God is like, and it is logical to believe that God did not overlook these other possibilities, or make a mistake in His choice. The typical Evangelical understanding of God is that He is omniscient, omnipotent, omnibenevolent, and omnisapient,[30] and is therefore incapable of error in any fashion, therefore, children being born of parents into a family structure, had to be His perfect choice and by His divine decree.

In Genesis 2:24 an interesting foreshadowing takes place. "Therefore a man shall leave his father and his mother and hold fast to his wife, and they shall become one flesh." Before there was a "father or mother," the family structure is assumed. At this point, there were two people on the face of the earth, Adam and Eve, and yet the family structure is addressed. Many understand

[30]. Norman Geisler, *Systematic Theology Volume Two: God and Creation* (Minneapolis, Minnesota: Bethany House, 2005). Geisler does an excellent job in Part One of revealing God's attributes.

that this is most likely commentary added by Moses to shed some light as to the reason for creating Eve, and how the family structure would eventually function,[31] but it is still interesting how early in the Scripture the concept of family arises. From this first mention in Genesis until the revealing of the Church Bride in Revelation 21, the concepts of family, marriage, and childbearing permeate the Scripture.

When the all-knowing God considered all of the options available for humankind, the family model was chosen above all others. God determined that one man, one woman, and as many children as these two would conceive, comprised the best method for reproduction, overall human development, spiritual enlightenment, and the unveiling of His purposes. In addition, as will be covered in detail later, God clearly instructed the parents (delegated to them) to assure that their offspring would learn and follow His commands.

When God chose to reveal Himself to the human race, He chose a specific title. Many were available to Him such as, president, emperor, potentate, CEO, ruler, chief, and monarch, but He chose the personal title "Father."[32] By not choosing the others, even though God is far greater than any of those earthly titles, God forever bound Himself to familial language and all that it entails. Family language stirs up thoughts of intimate relationships, blood ties, life-long entanglements, commitment, responsibility, and exclusiveness. Earthly parents have faults, and some are even abusive, but God as Father is perfect without defect. Evangelicals freely use statements like, "God is our Father," and "Jesus is our Brother," in sermons and songs, thus reinforcing the family concept. As believers we are "born again" into a new family with God as our Father, and every other

---

[31]. John E. Hartley, *The New International Biblical Commentary - Genesis* (Peabody, Ma: Hendrickson Publishers, 2000), 63.
[32]. Walter A. Elwell, *Evangelical Dictionary of Theology* (Grand Rapids, MI: Baker Books, 1984), 461.

believer is considered as our brother and sister. We are forever referred to as God's children, and for all eternity, we will be the Bride of Christ. The family metaphor/model is referenced extensively in the pages of Scripture including the historical, poetical, prophetical, and even apocalyptical literature genres contained within.

As stated, it is evident from even a casual reading of the Holy Scripture that the family is, and remains, primary in God's purposes for humankind. It is within the framework of the family system that Christianity is demonstrated, and the reality of its impact is either reinforced, or exposed as wanting. From the beginning of the Scriptures, the family is revealed as central in God's dealings with humankind, and throughout the multiple books, family relationships dominate its pages. From God dealing with Israel as family groups, to revealing Himself as Father, the family model is central. It is beyond the scope of this book to develop fully the number of Scriptures that directly or indirectly mention the family's role in society, for there are thousands, so that task will have to be left for the Christian sociologists to research. However, several key passages will be examined from both Testaments, concerning the role of the parents in the spiritual development of the next generation.

First, consider the often-neglected genealogies of the Scriptures. In Genesis 5, the tracing of lineage from Adam to Noah is revealed. In Genesis 11, Shem's descendants and Terah's lineage leading to Abraham is covered. Both Testaments are sprinkled with these seemingly endless lists of unpronounceable names, including priests, kings, and, there are even two for the Lord Jesus Himself. It is not necessary to develop all of them, for there are dozens. Each of them is important, and each consumes precious space in God's Word, so they are included for a specific purpose. Assuredly, each of these lists serves many additional goals, but the one to focus on currently is that of the family connection. The family lineage entitled a person to property ownership rights, inheritance, and the path to the throne.[33] In addition, this list proved that the people were part of something far greater than just themselves. In our culture, where the majority of one's time and energy seems focused on the individual, this may seem strange. However, in Biblical culture, family connections were of utmost importance. Family connections mattered greatly, and were valued so much that these long lists of names would be memorized and passed on for centuries. Knowing if someone was from Levi was important for example, for he alone could serve in the service of the tabernacle (Deuteronomy 10:8). Of course, Jesus had to be from the line of King David in order to be the Messiah and fulfill prophecy, thus the reason that His lineage is traced back to King David in Matthew 1. In addition, Jesus' family line is traced back to Adam in Luke 3 to assure the reader that He is the savior of all humankind, not just the Jewish nation.[34] Genealogies are important reminders of who these people were, and where their place was in history. These lists provided a family connection to generations gone by, and provided an anchor for those living in the current one.

Most Bible readers will be familiar with the story of Moses and the wanderings in the desert for forty years. One important story is that of Korah's rebellion in Numbers 16. What is interesting, beyond the ground opening up and swallowing them, is that God not only kills Korah for his rebellion, but also his entire family, thus implying that family connections are important from a negative point of view as well as positive. God often did not divide the families, and many times, the actions of the father had tremendous ramifications to the remaining members of his clan. It would be very difficult to read the Scripture and not discover family connections or related

---

[33]. Hartley, *The New International Biblical Commentary - Genesis*, 91.

[34]. Evans, Craig A, *The New International Biblical Commentary - Luke* (Peabody, Ma: Hendrickson Publishers, 1998), 58.

consequences, either good or bad. Cain and Abel, Noah and the Flood, David and Goliath, Joseph and his brothers, Moses; everyone is interconnected, and their actions affected their families. The Tribes of Israel camped by families, and the heads of those families are often involved in the narrative.

This general discussion could go on for hundreds of pages, but for now, it is sufficient to say that the importance of the family in the Scripture cannot be overstated. The pages of Old Testament Scripture are abundantly packed with family related stories that are both successful and dismal. These historical narratives underscore the centrality of the family unit, and highlight the role of the family in passing on values, education, and the faith.

Moving From the General to Specific

From the previous general comments, now let us consider some specific verses regarding the importance of the family and its role in passing on faith from parents to children.

> Genesis 18:19 - For I have chosen him, that he may command his children and his household after him to keep the way of the LORD by doing righteousness and justice, so that the LORD may bring to Abraham what He has promised him.

In this early passage dealing with the covenantal promise to Abraham, God not only mentions Abraham but also his children and household. God seems to tie the fulfillment of the covenant with Abraham's responsibility to impart an understanding of "the way of the Lord" to his family. The words, "so that" seem to imply a cause and effect action. If Abraham is faithful to train his children and household to "keep the way of the Lord," then God will bring the promise. It is not known what would have happened if Abraham had failed to command his children, but it can be clearly recognized the importance of doing so. At this point, it is sufficient to understand that God *expected* Abraham to command and train his household in the ways of the Lord.

A few representative verses in the Law demonstrate how God specifically commanded parents to train their children, and placed an equal burden on the children to learn from their parents.

Part of Moses' instruction to his followers before they crossed into the Promise Land, included specific commands to parents.

> Deuteronomy 4:9: - Only take care, and keep your soul diligently, lest you forget the things your eyes have seen, and lest they depart from your heart all the days of your life. Make them known to your children and your children's children.

Adam Clarke's comments on this verse are interesting:

> On family religion, God lays much stress; and no head of a family can neglect it without endangering the final salvation of his own soul.[35]

Clarke ties the very salvation of the individual to the efforts of the head of the home to instruct those under their leadership. While not venturing into the underlying theological issues with that statement, it does point out how much emphasis both God and Clarke placed on passing on faith to the next generation. God expected parents to "make them known" to their children and grandchildren. This responsibility was not and could not be delegated to anyone else.

---

[35]. Adam Clarke, "Deuteronomy," in *Adam Clark's Commentary on the Bible*.

Deuteronomy 6:4-9 are key verses both to the Jewish nation and to Christians.

> Hear, O Israel: The LORD our God, the LORD is one. You shall love the LORD your God with all your heart and with all your soul and with all your might. And these words that I command you today shall be on your heart. You shall teach them diligently to your children, and shall talk of them when you sit in your house, and when you walk by the way, and when you lie down, and when you rise. You shall bind them as a sign on your hand, and they shall be as frontlets between your eyes. You shall write them on the doorposts of your house and on your gates.

Beginning with the famous, "Hear O Israel," and ending with "write them on your doorposts," this passage of Scripture clearly reinforces the importance and breadth of parental responsibility to teach the next generation. The joining of loving your Lord God with everything you have, and commanding the teaching of these "words" diligently to our children, is a powerful combination. Clearly, part of what God expects of parents is the impartation of personal faith to the next generation.

These verses in Deuteronomy during the late 1970's and early 1980's launched a movement that is still growing in our day.[36] The home education movement was birthed by parents taking these challenging words seriously. The above verses were quoted in almost every gathering by the early pioneers of this group. The breadth of this command is staggering if taken literally. "When you sit, when you walk, when you lie down and when you arise," does not leave a great deal of time for much else. Many

---

[36]". Homeschooling Research," October, 2008, http://www.hslda.org/research/faq.asp (accessed October 2, 2008). Estimates range from 1.9 to 2.5 million home-educated students in 2003.

interpreted this verse to mean if one is lying down or arising is similar to "only when you are alone or with someone." The point is clear that God wanted his people to make sure to tell their children of His wonderful acts and ways. While a study of the home education movement is a worthwhile endeavor, it is beyond the scope of this book. However, the movement itself does reflect the understanding of how broad and how serious of a command these verses are to parents in reaching the next generation for Christ. In addition, many of those same parents do not believe that this responsibility can be delegated to the Church or to Christian Schools. Often, home school families shun both the school and the youth ministries offered by their local church. This rejection of the Church's training efforts is not meant to be disrespectful, but an honest attempt to fulfill what is believed to be a God-given, undelegatable command.

Charles Colson, in his book, *Against the Night, Living in the New Dark Ages* presents the belief system of many of these parents in the following quote:

> Ordained by God as the basic unit of human organization, the family is not only necessary for propagating the race, but is the first school of human instruction. ...No other structure can replace the family. Without it, our children have no moral foundation. Without it, they become moral illiterates whose only law is self.[37]

W. F. Adeney captures the thought process of these parents in this quote: "The parent is the spiritual guardian of his children. He cannot delegate to another the responsibility that God will someday call him to account for."[38] The result of this

---

[37]. Charles Colson, and Ellen Santilli Vaughn, *Against The Night: Living in The New Dark Ages* (Grand Rapids, Michigan: Zondervan, 1999), 77.

[38]. W. F. Adeney, "Deuteronomy," in *The Pulpit Commentary*

philosophical mindset is that sometimes there is tension between families that home educate their children and the organized church that is program oriented. The parents are attempting to fulfill what they believe is expected by God and often choose not to participate in the church's activities, which can be viewed as not being loyal or supportive to the vision of the church. The intersection of the role of the Church and the family will be examined later, so it will not be developed here, but suffice it to say, that there is sometimes conflict in the understanding of the roles of both the family and the church which can lead to tension.

During the transference of leadership from Moses to Joshua, the former instructs his successor on how to celebrate the Feast of Booths in Deuteronomy 31:12-13:

> Assemble the people, men, women, and little ones, and the sojourner within your towns, that they may hear and learn to fear the Lord your God, and be careful to do all the words of this law, and that their children, who have not known it, may hear and learn to fear the Lord your God, as long as you live in the land that you are going over the Jordan to possess.

The separation of the family into its various parts by age grouping is not the Biblical norm, and this verse would imply the same. The "little ones" were to be included in the celebration of this feast with no provision made to separate or isolate them away from the family celebration. This verse would have been an excellent opportunity for Moses to instruct his apprentice on how to deal with the multitude of children that could be potentially disruptive to the religious gathering. Moses did not take that opportunity in this passage or anywhere else in his written instructions. This passage certainly does not negate the

(Electronic Edition STEP Files; reprint, AGES Library, 2007).

usage of age-segregation techniques, but neither is it suggested or demonstrated. The sheer multitude of children present at any religious gathering would have presented many opportunities for Moses to address the issue, but he does not, and never does.

Through the progression of Scripture, we are allowed to observe Joshua's adherence to the commands received from Moses. As Joshua gathered all the people of Israel to Mount Ebal to renew the covenant, he read the entire Book of the Law. Notice those present at this reading in the following verse, Joshua 8:35:

> There was not a word of all that Moses commanded that Joshua did not read before all the assembly of Israel, and the women, and the little ones, and the sojourners who lived among them.

It must have been important to Joshua to include the women and children in the hearing of the Law for they were all present. Since both blessings and curses were contained within the Law, (8:34) the entire family needed to understand the depth of the commands with its rewards and warnings. In the future, God would hold parents responsible for the actions of their children, and specifically issue judgments based on their behavior. While not recorded, it is assumed that the parents would be required to explain some, if not much, of what was read by Joshua to their children. If Joshua read, "all that Moses commanded," there would be some very interesting conversations ahead. J. C. Ryle asserts, "Any system of training that does not make knowledge of Scripture the first thing is unsafe and unsound."[39] The Scripture points out that the "little ones" were present, and again, it would have been an excellent time to present some instruction of how to deal with them. That instruction is not

---

[39]. J. C. Ryle, "Primary Obligation of Parents," *Free Grace Broadcaster* 208 (Summer 2008), 12.

there, leading to a conclusion that their presence was considered a normal part of the religious life.

Joel 2:15-16 depicts an interesting gathering that seemed representative of what was common in the Old Testament experience.

> Blow a trumpet in Zion; consecrate a fast; call a solemn assembly; gather the people. Consecrate the congregation; assemble the elders; gather the children, even nursing infants.

Every member of the family was called upon and expected to participate in this "solemn assembly," including children and babies. The congregation included all ages.

While there are many such verses, one more will suffice to make clear the Bible's emphasis on including the entire family. During the reign of Hezekiah, while he was restoring the service of the temple, priests were being gathered and registered. Notice that the enrollment was tied to their fathers' house, and also notice *who was enrolled* in the following verses - 2 Chronicles 31:17-18:

> The enrollment of the priests was according to their fathers' houses; that of the Levites from twenty years old and upward was according to their offices, by their divisions. They were enrolled with all their little children, their wives, their sons, and their daughters, the whole assembly...

All of the preceding verses imply that the family was not segregated into differing age brackets during religious gatherings. Whether reading the words of Moses, celebrating religious festivals, or even fasting, children and infants were present and were, in fact, commanded to be so.

The Consequences of Failing to Impart Faith

All parents are an example for their children. If God commanded the parents to instruct their children, and He held them responsible for that command, then the Scripture should provide examples of the successes and failures of this command. It does. What follows is an examination of negative training demonstrated in the Scripture, and how this behavior hinders the transference of faith into the next generation. Richard Fugate states this negative training principle well, "You set the standards for his acceptable conduct either by what you allow (training by default) or by what you intentionally teach (overt negative training)."[40]

While parents often delegate their responsibilities to others, God ultimately holds the parents responsible for their children and for their spiritual development. Moreover, the example set by the parents is critical to that development. Even secular agencies recognize this Biblical truth. Linda Schuchmann, writing an article for Boys Town, states,

> Social learning scientists have shown that much of learning that occurs during development is acquired through observation and imitation. When asked, most of us would agree that children learn from role models and imitate behaviors of those they admire. The question then is not, "Do children imitate adults?" But, "Which behaviors of adults do children imitate?" And, "How can we make it more likely they will imitate positive versus negative behaviors?"[41]

[40]. J. Richard Fugate, *What The Bible Says About Child Training*, Second ed. (Apache Junction, Arizona: Foundation For Biblical Research, 1999), 72.

[41]. Linda Schuchmann, "Rolemodeling for Children," 2008, Boys

The Scripture is replete with examples of parental failure and its dire consequences, and there is not sufficient space to address them all. The first family of Adam and Eve had the ultimate sibling rivalry, which resulted in murder. Lot could not convince his son-in-laws to leave Sodom, and it appears that Sodom did not leave his daughters either, since they both had an immoral relationship with their father. Abraham had his Ishmael, and Jacob had twelve sons that were not exactly a close family unit. Skipping forward in time a few centuries Eli, who had the dubious distinction of having sons referred to as "worthless men" in 1 Samuel 2:12, is encountered. The Lord was not at all pleased with how Eli had raised his sons, so He called a young man named Samuel to replace him in service. We know the story of the dreams and voices, but the reason for Eli's rejection is worth looking at for our purposes. God explains to Samuel in 1 Samuel 3:13-14:

> And I declare to him that I am about to punish his house forever, for the iniquity that he knew, because his sons were blaspheming God, and he did not restrain them. Therefore I swear to the house of Eli that the iniquity of Eli's house shall not be atoned for by sacrifice or offering forever.

From the surrounding verses, it is apparent that the sons of Eli were adults, for their sins were not ones typically committed by children, *yet* God held Eli responsible for their actions, at least for not dealing with the sins in a public fashion. Eli's failure permanently cost his "house" the priesthood.

Samuel was raised by Eli and regretfully, Samuel apparently

Town,
http://www.parenting.org/guidance/rolemodelingforchildren.asp (accessed September 19, 2008).

did not learn from Eli's mistakes, for his son's sins cost his "house" the right to rule over Israel, thus ushering in the monarchy of Israel.

> 1 Samuel 8:4-5: Then all the elders of Israel gathered together and came to Samuel at Ramah and said to him, "Behold, you are old and your sons do not walk in your ways. Now appoint for us a king to judge us like all the nations.

Samuel's failure as a father led to Israel rejecting God and asking for a king. Poor parenting can have significant consequences including a loss of everything the parents attempted to gain throughout their lifetime. Consider this brief, but sad trail of failure though the kings of Israel and Judah: Solomon produced Rehoboam, Jehoshaphat produced Jehoram, Hezekiah produced Manasseh, and Josiah produced Jehoahaz. Solomon, Jehoshaphat, Hezekiah, and Josiah were major reformers who brought a godly revival to their nation, yet their children were wicked and destroyed everything that their fathers had accomplished. All of the good works were lost within one generation. The changes made by the godly were undone by the next generation. Somehow, these godly men, who had changed a nation, were not successful in reaching their own children, and all of their labors were lost. Parental failure to impart their own faith into the children led to much heartache and devastation.

Pertaining to my thinking is the noticeable absence of any judgment, condemnation, or correction specifically in reference to the organized religious community. The blame rested on the parents.

The Blessings of Imparting Faith

On the positive side, there are examples of children that

walked in the commands of their parents, and adopted their parent's faith. One stellar example is the story of the Rechabites revealed in Jeremiah 35. Jeremiah was instructed by God to bring the sons of Jonadab into the temple and offer them wine. They refused to drink because of a command from Jonadab given almost three hundred years previously. It seems that both God and Jeremiah marveled, and God used this obedience to highlight the gross disobedience of Judah. The final words of the chapter should offer great encouragement to fathers, "Therefore thus says the Lord of hosts, the God of Israel: Jonadab the son of Rechab shall never lack a man to stand before me." Apparently, the diligence of Jonadab to instruct his children paid dividends, forever. What he said, or however this father communicated his wishes, the point is that the children and grandchildren understood it clearly, and continued to hold fast to them, even in the face of a mighty prophet. In addition, these descendants refused to live in cities, but remained tent-dwellers, thus avoiding many of the difficulties associated with the repeated wars suffered by Judah. The decision not to build houses was also passed on by their ancestor.

C. S. Lewis remarks, "Aristotle says that the aim of education is to make the pupil like and dislike what he ought."[42] Jonadab was successful in making his pupils "dislike" wine, and "like" his instruction. In the end, these descendants were not only blessed by God, but also used by Him to promote instruction to the rest of the nation and down even into our day. Lewis also states,

> Each generation exercises power over its successors; and each, in so far as it modifies the environment bequeathed to it and rebels against tradition, resists and limits the power of its predecessors.[43]

---

[42]. C. S. Lewis, *The Abolition of Man* (San Francisco, CA: Harper Collins Publishers, 1944), 16.

[43]. Ibid., 56.

If the descendents of Jonadab had ignored their ancestor's instructions, they would have limited his power of example, and cut off the blessing of the promise of God "to always have someone serving Him." Concerning the current chapter, one key factor to notice is that the decisions made were based on the father's commands and do not reflect any influence from the religious community. In fact, in spite of the enticement from the religious system represented by Jeremiah and the temple setting, the father's commands were preferred and obeyed.

Further Old Testament Considerations

Consider the plethora of verses contained within the book of Proverbs dealing with family matters. A reprint of a significant portion of the book would have to be listed to delineate all of the verses that deal with parent/child, or husband/wife relationships. The main purpose of the Book was an attempt by a father to pass on wisdom to his children. Proverbs 1:8 – "Hear, my son, your father's instruction, and forsake not your mother's teaching." It seems that much of what Solomon learned he learned at his father's feet, Proverbs 4:3-5:

> When I was a son with my father, tender, the only one in the sight of my mother, he taught me and said to me, "Let your heart hold fast my words; keep my commandments, and live. Get wisdom; get insight; do not forget, and do not turn away from the words of my mouth."

Could this be the reason that Solomon asked for wisdom from God when God appeared to him in a dream and promised him anything he desired in 1 Kings 3? It would seem at least to play into the decision. David invested in Solomon, and Solomon wrote the bulk of Proverbs to invest in his many sons. Solomon was modeling that fathers need to invest in their children, so when presented with opportunities to make important decisions, they would have a better chance of choosing well. Unfortunately, Solomon did not impart to his son Rehoboam much wisdom, as evidenced by his selfish and unwise choice made in 1 Kings 12. When seeking counsel, Rehoboam chose to listen to his peers instead of his father's counselors, and the nation ended up in division.

Some believe that Rehoboam's choice was a negative result of the effect of youth ministry, but this is a stretch of the text. However, Proverbs does offer insight into the selection of friends. Proverbs 13:20 – "Whoever walks with the wise becomes wise, but the companion of fools will suffer harm." Rehoboam would have been wiser to walk with the older men, instead of the foolish companions of his youth. John Angell James correctly believed:

One ill-chosen friend of your children's may undo all the good you are the means of doing at home. It is impossible for you to be sufficiently vigilant on this point.[44]

"You win, or lose by the friends you choose," goes a common, sagely rhyme. Rehoboam and Israel lost a great deal by the choosing of poor friendships.

In Proverbs 3:11-12 observe the oft-used comparison of God's discipline and that of a human father. Throughout Proverbs, and again in Hebrews 12, we find God's hand of restraint, discipline, and even corporal punishment, compared to a loving human father's role.

The image of a loving father is used instead of any corporate or organizational symbol of power or restraint.

Before leaving the Old Testament, the last Book has some interesting verses. Malachi spoke the final words from God that Israel would experience for 400 years. Like so many prophets, Malachi is a mixture of hope and rebuke from God to His people. There is a clear delineation between the religious and family structure within this book. The priests were rebuked for offering polluted animals on the altar (1:7-8) and for violating their marriage vows (2:14-15). An interesting fact about God's reason for hating divorce, is the direct correlation between this vow- breaking, and the impact on the children in 2:15, "And what was the one God seeking? Godly offspring." The impact of divorce on the next generation is well documented in our day, but it must have been known in Malachi's also. God hated divorce, and He equated it with "covering a garment with violence." The priests were being rebuked by God for divorcing their wives, and the primary concern of God, was the impact being made on the next generation.

---

44. John Angell James, Principle Obstacles in Bringing Up Children for Christ," 39.

The last book of the Old Testament ends with a promise and a curse; both are concerned with the family relationship. Malachi 4:5:6:

> Behold, I will send you Elijah the prophet before the great and awesome day of the Lord comes. And he will turn the hearts of fathers to their children and the hearts of children to their fathers, lest I strike the land with a decree of utter destruction.

This promise and curse would be the final word of God for four centuries. It is understood from Jesus' words that John Baptist was Elijah, but what does the hearts of the fathers and children being turned mean. While not expounded in the text, it surely *at least means* that the family relationship is extremely important, and should be a primary focus of God's people, as well as a pursuit of ministry for the Church.

Since so much was covered in this chapter, let me briefly summarize. In this chapter, consideration was given to several Old Testament verses and concepts that clearly present a picture of the primacy of the family in God's plan for reaching the next generation. From genealogies and general concepts, to a refusal to drink wine and disobedient sons, the family model is primary in the Scriptural pattern. There is nothing referenced in any of the narratives, which would lead one to assume that outside religious sources had a major impact in the impartation of faith into the next generation. This does not necessarily forbid using methods not recorded in the Old Testament; however, the point is that they are not mentioned. The actions, or lack thereof, of the parents were the *primary* factor revealed in reference to the impartation of the faith (or not) into the children. In addition, there are no Old Testament references to any segregation of ages specifically dealing with the family. Children, infants, and adults lived together, heard the Scripture together, and sometimes even died together. There are references in the Old Testament that refer to age requirements, for the priesthood and qualifications for military service, but these had nothing to do with the transference of faith generationally.

Next Stop:

In the next chapter, some New Testament verses and concepts will be presented pertaining to the imparting of faith to the next generation. In addition, several insightful quotes from scholars will be examined.

4 THE VIEW FROM THE NEW TESTAMENT

In the previous chapter, Deuteronomy 6 was referred to as containing a foundational set of verses for the home education movement. These verses were often coupled with Ephesians 6:4 "Fathers, do not provoke your children to anger, but bring them up in the discipline and instruction of the Lord." In the early 1980's, many young fathers were attempting to understand what this verse meant specifically in reference to their responsibly in the home. These men wanted to know how to accomplish God's will in this verse, understanding that the responsibility landed on their shoulders, and that there did not seem to be any way to remove it, or delegate it away Biblically. This understanding of the father's responsibility was commonly accepted in previous generations, but in ours, it seems displaced. David Martyn Lloyd-Jones, in a sermon entitled, *Nurture and Admonition,* captures the sentiment clearly,

> This is the emphasis throughout the Bible. It is not something that is to be handed over to the school, however good the school may be.

It is the duty of parents - their primary and most essential duty.[45]

Later in the same sermon, Jones adds:

> The home is the fundamental unit of society; and children are born into a home, into a family. There you have the circle that is to be the chief influence in their lives. There is no question about that. It is the biblical teaching everywhere, and it is always in so-called civilizations where ideas concerning the home begin to deteriorate that society ultimately disintegrates.[46]

Jones' words are clearly applicable today. Western civilization is in moral free fall, and the bottom is yet to be reached. Richard Baxter was an English Puritan preacher with some very clear views on the responsibility of the parents in imparting faith to the next generation:

> Wicked parents are the most notable servants of the devil in all the world and the bloodiest enemies to their children's souls. More souls are damned by God through the influences of ungodly parents – the next to them...ungodly ministers and magistrates- than by any instruments in the world besides.[47]

The language of Baxter is not common anymore, but the reality of the belief by earlier generations that the responsibility of the

---

[45]. David Martyn Lloyd-Jones, "Nurture and Admonition," *Free Grace Broadcaster* 208 (Summer 2008), 6.

[46]. Ibid., 7.

[47]. Richard Baxter, "Biblical Parenthood," *Free Grace Broadcaster* 208 (Summer 2008), 32.

parents was significant, cannot be overstated. Baxter's quote places the greatest amount of judgment on the parents, and then on the other authorities by mentioning both ministers and the government magistrates, when the next generation does not follow in the previous' footsteps. Since the bulk of a child's time is spent with their parents, their influence will be far greater than either ministers or magistrates.

In all of these quotes, and in the Biblical text used so far, the parents are the primary source of instruction, and ultimately the ones held responsible for the impartation of faith into the next generation. The family functioning together, worshipping together, and maintaining the same value system was the normal pattern presented in Scripture.

However, this family picture is not the usual one experienced in our day. David Wells astutely states,

> Families that function together, and that do so with a set of common moral values, are becoming an endangered species. Families have traditionally served as the chief conduit for the transmission of values from one generation to another, and now this conduit is breaking down.[48]

In fairness, the absence of mentioning age-segregation in Scripture does not necessarily disqualify its usage as a viable model, but it does raise some questions as to its current prominence in the modern, Evangelical church. However, Schaeffer states well the freedom to disagree on these points:

> It is my thesis that as we cannot bind men morally except with that which the Scripture clearly commands (beyond that we can only give advice), similarly, anything the New

---

[48]. David F. Wells, *God in the Wasteland; The Reality of Truth in a World of Fading Dreams* (Grand Rapids, MI: Eerdmans, 1994), 14.

Testament does not command in regard to church form is a freedom to be exercised under the leadership of the Holy Spirit for that particular time and place.[49]

Freedom is a tremendous gift, but it must be balanced with Paul's caution in 1 Corinthians 10:23, "All things are lawful, but not all things are profitable. All things are lawful, but not all things edify." Just because a method is not mentioned in the Scripture, it does not disqualify its usage.

Nevertheless, the other side is also true; just because a method is used, it does not make it Biblical.

A New Testament Successful Parent

A wonderful, often overlooked example of parental success is Philip, an early church deacon. Because of persecution by Saul, the early church was spread out all over the countryside, and Philip was one of those thrust out of his hometown. Philip found himself in Samaria and a major revival soon broke out. In the midst of this revival, an angel appeared to Philip and told him to leave this work and go south towards Gaza. The story is well known - Philip met an influential man reading the Scriptures, led him to Christ, baptized him, and then (perhaps) literally flew away. All of the details are recorded by Luke in Acts chapter 8, but that is not the last recorded information about Philip. Philip is encountered again in Acts 21:7-9:

> On the next day we departed and came to Caesarea, and we entered the house of Philip the evangelist, who was one of the seven, and stayed with him. He had four unmarried daughters, who prophesied.

---

[49]. Schaeffer, *The Church At The End of The 20th Century*, 76.

This same Saul, now Paul, that had driven Philip out of town by persecution, was staying with him in Caesarea as a dearly beloved brother in Christ. What is interesting is that Philip left a major revival in Samaria, led someone to Christ by divine appointment, ended up in the city of Caesarea, and was still there many years later. It is not recorded as to everything that Philip did there, and we do not know if he struggled with regretting the fact that he had to leave a revival. What is recorded is that he seemed to have flourished, and so did his family. Philip was known as "the evangelist" indicating what he did with his time, and important to this study, he had four grown daughters that followed the Lord. Philip remains one of the Biblical heroes because he clearly demonstrated how to "bloom where he was planted." In addition, Philip displayed the willingness to keep walking with the Lord and not become stuck in the "good old days." So many people seem to live in wasted regret of what the Lord *used* to do, instead of participating in what God *is* currently doing. Philip invested in his city and as important, for this book, his family. Philip successfully passed on his faith to his four grown daughters, while reaching the lost for Christ right where he lived.

Additional New Testament Considerations

There are several other family considerations given significant space in the New Testament writings. From a negative point of view, the disobedience of children is listed as a sign of the end of the age, and a disqualification for elders serving in church leadership. On the positive side, large sections of Scripture are dedicated to marriage and family matters, and these give insight into their importance to the Church and society.

The centrality of the family and its importance to the Church simply cannot be overstated. David Wells states,

The small social units made up of family and place...are now clogged or broken. The young are cut loose to drift in the sea of impersonal society. How will they learn about life, and what will they learn?[50]

Wells laments in the same quotation that families served as the, "chief conduits for the transmission of values from one generation to another." Wells correctly believes that the Scriptures teach that where the family is dysfunctional, the Church will soon follow. When the Church becomes unable to effectively communicate the power of the Gospel in the home, society quits paying attention to Her message.

The Apostle Paul liked to write lists. Several of his letters are populated with long, run-on sentences that contain line upon line of lists of sins. The end of Romans 1 is such a place. After addressing man's spiral downward into depravity, Paul presents a list of sins that God will "give them up to" ending in a debased mind. This list begins with, "filled with all manner of unrighteousness," and ends with "ruthless." Notice that, "disobedient to parents" is included in the list that also contains, "murder, haters of God, and inventors of evil." God's view of this type of behavior however, seems to be clear in verse 32: "Though they know God's decree that those who practice such things deserve to die..." Few in our current cultural mindset, would equate murder with disobedience to parents, and even less would dispense the same penalty – death. However, God does make that connection, and this is not the only place He does so.

In 2 Timothy 3:1-7, "disobedient to their parents" is included in another list of horrid sins including, "hateful, unholy, heartless, brutal, and those that do not love God." Apparently, God considers children that are disobedient to their parents to

---

[50]. David F. Wells, *No Place for Truth, Or Whatever Happened to Evangelical Theology?* (Grand Rapids, MI: Eerdmans Publishing, 1993), 156.

be living in serious sin. A theological study of Original Sin is beyond the scope of this book, but most Evangelicals, as well as those of the Roman Catholic faith, would accept the premise that children are born with it.[51] We do not completely understand how this mysterious transference of sin takes place, but we deal with its ravages every day. Most parents know that they do not have to train their children to lie, cheat, or steal, they come already well versed in such behavior. Ryle wrote, "Remember children are born with a decided bias towards evil. Therefore, if you let them choose for themselves, they are certain to choose wrong."[52] God expects parents to train their children to obey, and if they are not trained, the parents are responsible, and the results can be devastating.

As previously mentioned in Ephesians 6:4, God commands fathers to "bring them up in the Lord." Preceding this verse is a command directed to the children. "Children obey your parents in everything, for this is right." Parents are instructed to teach and train, and children are commanded to listen and obey. When this process is followed, the transference of wisdom and faith from one generation to the next can take place. When it is not adhered to, we have societal breakdown. It would not be too great of a stretch to state that our society is in the breakdown stage. To quote Wells again,

> The family once served as the chief conduit for this transmission, but the family is now collapsing, not merely because of divorce but as a result of affluence and the innovations of a technological age.[53]

Based on the studies referenced in chapter one, the Church is also struggling with the passing on of values, morals, as well as

---

51. Elwell, *Evangelical Dictionary of Theology*, 1013.

52. Ryle, Primary Obligation of Parents," 11.

53. Wells, *No Place for Truth, Or Whatever Happened to Evangelical Theology?* 84.

faith to the next generation. Children that are not *trained* to be obedient will struggle to receive from their parents the necessary truths to accept the Christian faith. Michael Pearl, a child-training author and speaker, puts it well, "Parents must assume that part of the child's moral duty which is not yet fully developed."[54] Until the child is old enough to understand self-control for example, the parents must provide that control.

God expects parents to train their children, and He commands the children to obey. This issue was so important that Paul included it in both sets of instructions concerning the selection of elders.

In 1 Timothy 3 and Titus 1, Paul gives specific instructions to his mentorees detailing the importance of the leader's family. What is interesting is that Paul only expanded one aspect of the necessary qualities mentioned – how the proposed elder led his family. "For if someone does not manage his own household, how will he care for God's church?" Paul asks in 1 Timothy 3:5. "Above reproach," "sober-minded," "not quarrelsome," and even, "able to teach," could all have been expanded, but only," he must manage his household well," is.

Managing his own household provides insight into how this potential elder will lead the family of God. The leader's abilities will be reflected in his own home. Specifically, revealed in "how his children submit," and in Titus, that his children are, "believers, and not open to the charge of debauchery or insubordination."

How the elder trained his children to obey his authority is representative of how this man will lead the church. Unfortunately, this requirement is often lacking in the families that lead the Church, and represent the Church on the mission field. Stereotypical jokes and language are often exaggerated, but in many of them, there is a grain of truth. "PK's" and "MK's"

---

54. Michael Pearl, *To Train Up a Child* (Pleasantville, Tennessee: Michael Pearl Publishing, 1994), 18.

are often the subject of these type jokes, and there is an element of truth contained within them. Historically, the responsibility of controlling, training, and imparting faith into the next generation rested on the shoulders of the father. His success or failure would qualify, or disqualify him for service in leading the Church. All too rarely, it seems, is this principle followed in our day.

The family structure is also addressed in several other passages: Ephesians 5 provides details on the proper husband and wife relationship. 1 Corinthians 7 sheds light on marriage, divorce, widows, and singles. Colossians 3 revisits the roles of husbands, wives, and children. Hebrews 12 compares God's discipline to an earthly father's, and 1 Peter 3 presents this apostle's understanding of family relationships. Peter even explains how a poor relationship between a husband and wife can hinder the effectiveness of the husband's prayers. Each of these sections of Scripture *could* be further developed to reinforce the point of the centrality of the family in God's plan for reaching the next generation for Christ, but will not be for the sake of brevity. However, these sections do reinforce the prominence of the family's place in the pages of New Testament Scripture.

Next Stop:

While we cannot spend the time necessary to develop each of the previous points, a godly marriage must be considered in our discussion of faith impartation. Chapter five will explore marriage and its impact on the next generation.

5 THE IMPORTANCE OF A GODLY MARRIAGE

A godly marriage is the first component necessary to help in the transference of the Christian value system to the next generation. The ideal is of course one man, one woman for life, both who are trying to follow the Lord with all their heart, soul, mind, and strength. Life is made up of less than ideal situations and therefore it is hard to generalize about marriage in our current day. One-parent homes and multiple divorces are the norm for our modern era, and this has taken a tremendous toll on our children. In this chapter however, we will be primarily discussing the traditional understanding of a Christian home, one father, one mother, and one or more children living in the home. The Biblical principles discussed are still relevant to a non-traditional home; they are just much harder to implement, and the damages caused by the destruction of the home are compounded on the next generation.

It has been stated, "If your Christianity does not work in the home, don't export it![55]" "Work," is defined in such things as being Christ-like to your spouse and children, walking in humility and forgiveness towards one another, demonstrating a genuine devotional life, praying together, learning how to give and receive

---

[55]. Jeffrey A. Klick, *Bumper Car Theology* (Morrisville, North Carolina: Lulu Publishing, 2006), 15.

correction and apologies, and developing relationships that will last for your lifetime. Biblical Christianity is not something we "do" on Sunday but has little meaning for the rest of our lives. Genuine, Biblical Christianity is demonstrated primarily in the home. If the people that know us the best cannot testify about the reality of our belief system, who possible could?

If our spouse, children, or siblings were to be interviewed, and guaranteed immunity from reprisals, what would they say about our Christianity? The power and reality of the Gospel should first be demonstrated in the home. One reason given by young people that reject their parents' value system and set of beliefs is hypocrisy in the home. "Christianity didn't do much for them, why should I accept it?" is often the prevailing comment. Husbands and wives that are living in a truce environment or worse yet, a battle zone, instead of living in "oneness" that God desires, present a picture of ineptness on God's part, and most young people seek genuineness, not empty words.

The Scriptural standard is clear for marriage and is stated in many places. Since this is not a book entirely devoted to Christian marriage, I will not go into great detail on the subject, but a foundational understanding is necessary to see how the parents' relationship influences the next generation. For the sake of brevity the entire quote will not be reproduced here, but consider some of the salient passages contained in Ephesians 5:22-32:

> Wives, submit to your own husbands, as to the Lord... Husbands, love your wives, as Christ loved the church and gave himself up for her...In the same way husbands should love their wives as their own bodies... "Therefore a man shall leave his father and mother and hold fast to his wife, and the two shall become one flesh."...
>
> However, let each one of you love his wife as himself, and

let the wife see that she respects her husband.

The "becoming one" process is often difficult, but it will provide insight into the reality of our relationship and dependence on Christ. Contained within these verses is a significant amount of sermon material, but more importantly, the guidelines necessary for a successful marriage. Terms like "submission" and "love" have been grossly distorted in our society, but the Bible does not shrink back from using them, and neither should evangelicals. In this passage, submission refers to willingness to line up under a leader similar to a volunteer army.[56] Unlike the army, the husband cannot demand submission, but earns it through loving those under their care.

Many wives confide during marriage counseling that they have little problem willingly lining up under (submitting to) a godly, loving husband who is attempting to love his wife as Christ loved the Church. If a husband has a genuine relationship with God, and is seeking His will daily, the vast majority of wives have little problem following his leadership. Husbands are given the key to success by being commanded three times in the above verses to love their wife. In addition, the husbands are given explicit instruction as to *how* to love their wife, which voids out any arguments from the husband as to ignorance.

Husbands are told to "love their wives as Christ loved the church" and the point is obvious. Husbands are to lay down their lives for their wives, and this encompasses a great deal more than physical death. Most honorable men would gladly die for their family physically, but it is much harder to live for their family on a daily basis. This type of "dying" is a daily occurrence and requires great grace and patience. Many Christian marriage books attempt to explain this process so the point will not be belabored here. A husband that is willing to die to himself rarely

---

[56]. W. E. Vine, *An Expository Dictionary of New Testament Words* (Old Tappan, NJ: Fleming H. Revell, 1966), 86.

has a problem with an unhappy wife.

The children that are raised in a home that is populated with a dying-to-self husband, and a wife that is willingly lining up under his authority, have a significantly better chance of embracing their parent's faith. On a similar topic, two Harvard sociologists conducted a survey in 1950, which proved to be 90% accurate, in determining whether five and six-year-olds would eventually become delinquent. This study was conducted before the "sexual revolution" and mass overthrow of parental authority in the 60's. The results of the study in this previous generation are certainly applicable to our study:

> They discovered that the four primary factors necessary to prevent delinquency are: the father's firm, fair, and consistent discipline; the mother's supervision and companionship during the day; the parent's demonstrated affection for each other and for the children; and the family's spending time together in activities where all participated.[57]

Applicable to this book is that the parents in this study, had a good marriage and apparently enjoyed spending time together, thus the children avoided rebellion and crime as they aged. Those children whose parents did not perform the above four tasks, had a significantly higher percentage of failure, thus highlighting the influence of the parents on the children's future behavior.

---

[57]. Sheldon and Eleanor Glueck, *Unraveling Juvenile Delinquency* (Cambridge, MS: Harvard University Press, 1950), 257.

Children Catch What Is Important

As parents demonstrate the reality of the Christian faith, and how it influences every aspect of life, children will catch what the parents really possess. The "do as I say not as I do" philosophy is a myth. Children will understand quickly what is actually important to the parents, and not simply what the parents say is vital. If a parent states that church attendance is essential, but rarely makes it to the service, the message being taught to the children is clear; church attendance means little.

The same is true for Bible study, outreach, and service to others, finances, and every other aspect of the Christian life. Children will grasp what is actually significant to the parents by how the couple spends their time, not necessarily what the parents simply purport to be important. Actions do indeed speak louder than words in the picture presented to children. John Angell James, an English Congregationalist minister wrote over one hundred and fifty years ago:

> Religion, by every Christian parent, is theoretically acknowledged to be the most important thing in the world. But if in practice the father appears a thousand times more anxious for the son to be a good scholar than a real Christian, and the mother more solicitous for the daughter to be a good dancer or musician than a child of God, they may teach what they like in the way of good doctrine, but they are not to look for genuine piety as the result.[58]

One of the best things any married couple can do for their children is learn how to love one another, and attempt to make

---

[58]. John Angell James, Principle Obstacles in Bringing Up Children for Christ," 35.

Christ the center of the home. The opposite is also true. If a Christian couple demonstrates hatred, disgust, disrespect, animosity, etc. towards one another, the children quickly learn that the parents' faith is ineffective and impotent to offer hope or change. It is not humanly possible for there to be a complete absence of problems in any home, regardless of how spiritually mature a couple may become. However, teaching children how to work *through* difficulties is important to their development. All couples have times of what is sometimes called, "intense fellowship." Frustrations, anger, disappointments, and pressure can cause harsh words and displays of the sinful nature that are sometimes scary.

Parents must learn how to seek forgiveness when they sin, and demonstrate to their children how to walk through relational difficulties.

Most children will grow up, marry, and begin their attempts at "becoming one," and they need training on how to navigate the often-choppy waters of marriage. Parents can gain insight into how they are doing in passing on their marriage skills, by listening to the conversations of their children. If a parent hears, "I don't ever want to get married" repeatedly, perhaps some more work is needed. If the child often talks about, "wanting to find a spouse" and "settle down and have a family just like mom and dad," then they are probably on the right track of imparting the value of a godly marriage.

The damage caused to the next generation through divorce is well documented, and does not need to be restated here.[59] Personal interaction with numerous teens and adults that are from a broken home, readily confirms what is well known, divorce causes destruction in the next generation. Many adults

---

[59]. David Duea, "Child and Family Guidance Center," 2008, http://www.cfgpc.org/impact.htm (accessed September 24, 2008). This is a sample website prepared to deal with the damage of divorce.

are still reeling from the divorce their parents went through decades ago, and this divorce cycle is often repeated in the children's marriages. Not only is there damage thrust upon the children when a divorce happens, but specifically regarding a Christian couple that divorces, the testimony of Christ is damaged. Paul, in the passage in Ephesians 5, makes a connection between a marriage of humans, and a picture of Christ and the Church. What all is entailed in this is beyond human understanding, but this much is clear, Christian marriages are under attack and they are breaking up in record numbers,[60] and the fallout to the next generation is immeasurable.

This book is not intended to become a lesson on spiritual warfare, but we at least need to consider that the Scripture clearly teaches that Christians have an adversary, and he hates the church. (See 2 Corinthians 2:11 and 1 Peter 5:8) The adversary is specifically targeting this picture of Christ and the Church by attempting to destroy Christian marriages, and is being quite successful. Not only do these attacks distort the supernatural picture, but also as an added bonus, the next generation is also adversely impacted. Based on studies like Barna's just quoted, it seems that the enemy is being very successful in his efforts because Christian marriages are being destroyed at an alarming rate often rivaling those of non-Christians.

---

[60]. George Barna, "New Marriage and Divorce Statistics Released," March 31, 2008, Barna Research Group, http://www.barna.org/flexpage.aspx?page (accessed September 24, 2008).

Next Stop:

In the next chapter, we will explore some additional concepts regarding the family and open up how the roles each member plays directly affects faith impartation.

6 THE ROLES OF THE FAMILY MEMBERS

In the Scripture, it is clear that God places the responsibility on the shoulders of the husband and father to lead his family. A quote of unknown origin, and one that is certainly challenging states, "God always holds those in authority responsible for the actions of those under their authority." With leadership comes responsibility and accountability. During the counseling of many pastors, husbands, and fathers it sometimes becomes clear that these men demand to be followed as a leader, yet they are not willing to expend the necessary death-to-self required to earn such a following.

Many men struggle with Bible memorization, but almost every Christian man knows these passages - 1 Corinthians 11:13 – "But I want you to understand that the head of every man is Christ, the head of a wife is her husband, and the head of Christ is God." And, Ephesians 5:23 – "For the husband is the head of the wife even as Christ is the head of the church, his body, and is himself its Savior." Even men with little Biblical understanding can usually quote Ephesians 5:22 – "Wives, submit to your own husbands, as to the Lord," even if they do not know where it is located, they know it is there.

These verses are true and they clearly teach that the man is the head of the family, and he is therefore responsible for what happens under his leadership. Many men have a clear understanding of the headship part, but often do not have quite as focused picture of *their* responsibility. Jesus makes it abundantly clear that true, Biblical leadership begins with taking a servant position. Matthew 20:25-26:

> But Jesus called them to him and said, "You know that the rulers of the Gentiles lord it over them, and their great ones exercise authority over them. It shall not be so among you. But whoever would be great among you must be your servant."

This command is true for fathers and husbands, as well as apostles. Respect is earned not demanded, and so is the ability to have followers, including a wife and children. Husbands and fathers have been placed in a position of authority by God; therefore, they bear the weight of the responsibility. However, those under their care can choose to follow or reject them based on how the leader leads.

A paraphrased thought from Ken Nair's challenging book entitled, *Discovering the Mind of a Woman*[61] goes something like this. As the leader of your home, how are those under your leadership doing? If you have been married five, ten, or fifteen years, is your wife better or worse by being under your leadership? The same question can be asked about the children under the father's care. Are they better or worse after being under this leader?

Another passage to consider further is 1 Peter 3:7:

Likewise, husbands, live with your wives in an

---

[61]. Ken Nair, *Discovering the Mind of a Woman* (Nashville, Tennessee: Thomas Nelson, 1995).

understanding way, showing honor to the woman as the weaker vessel, since they are heirs with you of the grace of life, so that your prayers may not be hindered.

The husband is specifically challenged to live with his wife in an understanding way, which places the responsibility on the man. Part of this understanding must be in attempting to grasp what the wife needs, how she thinks, what her dreams and visions are for the family, and a host of other thoughts. Peter even states that the prayers of the man can be hindered if they do not live in this fashion. Any parent that is praying for their children to carry on their faith must consider the ramifications of this verse.

Previously Ephesians 6:4 and Deuteronomy 6 were referenced, and these verses clearly address the father's responsibility to instruct and guide their children in the ways of God. Colossians 3:21 simply reinforces the task, "Fathers, do not exasperate your children, so that they will not lose heart." "Lose heart" and "not provoking your children to anger" implies that there are actions that can be taken that will damage the relationship between fathers and children. Many excellent child-training books are readily available that can be consulted as to how avoid these issues, so this concept will not developed here. For the purpose of this book, it is sufficient to realize that fathers have a tremendous responsibility to impart to the next generation the truths of God's Word by both their words and actions.

The Role of the Wife

As already noted in Ephesians 5, the wife has a significant role in the marriage, and thus in the process of reaching the next generation. The wife is given as a helpmeet (Genesis 2:18) to her husband, and part of what she does to assist is to respect him. Men need respect to have the courage to lead, and primarily this will come from the wife. If this need is not met at home, the man will find it somewhere else such as in work, friends, or sports.

Proverbs 14:1 – "The wisest of women builds her house, but folly with her own hands tears it down." What a wife says to her husband can produce life or death, build him up or tear him down, help him be a leader or neuter him spiritually.

Many women have shared that they wish their husbands would pray with them. In a follow up question, they are asked if they ever prayed as a couple at any time in their life. Usually they will reply that they *used* to pray, but then they stopped. What the woman does not understand, is that in counseling hundreds of men, it is clear why they stopped praying with their wife. What men will typically relate is that they used to pray with their wife and children, but then the wife made a comment, something like, "You call *that* a prayer?" or, "Is that it, that's *all* we are going to pray about?" While those questions may seem within the boundaries of reason, what is not realized is that the man just felt slapped by his wife, and it will take a while before he attempts to lead again. Not too many men like to be put down or made fun of in this arena, especially in front of the children. Men will take this "attack" as a lack of respect, and the typical response is to lock down spiritually. A wise woman will build her home by thanking her husband, and encouraging any prayer, no matter how trivial it may seem to her at the time. Like priming a pump, if the man feels safe in praying, he will pray more, and will develop "better" prayers as time passes. Personal observation and interaction with many couples, has confirmed that the wife's respect of her husband will typically unlock more mature behavior in the husband.

While not necessarily politically correct in our day, the following is Biblically accurate. As a wife willingly lines up under (submits) to her husband, she is demonstrating great faith to her children.

The story of the Roman centurion in Matthew 8:5-9 clearly

knits together faith and authority. This solider approaches Jesus with a request for healing, and Jesus graciously agrees to follow him. The solider states that Jesus does not need to come, just simply say the word, and his servant will be healed. The centurion's rationale is what is interesting in this story. "I too am a man under authority and I say to this one come, and he comes, and to another go, and he goes." This Roman clearly understood authority. Jesus makes a fascinating comment after the centurion leaves, "I have not seen such great faith in all of Israel." It would seem logical for Jesus to have said, "I have not seen such a great understanding of authority in all of Israel," but He did not say that. Jesus linked an understanding of being under authority with great faith.

It is not a stretch to state that a wife that willingly lines up under her husband's authority has to have faith in order to believe that God will protect her, provide for her, lead her, and bless her, for following an imperfect man. As the wife demonstrates this process to her children, she is training them for their future responsibility as well. Young men are learning how a godly wife follows her husband, and therefore he needs to use his authority wisely. Daughters are being given training on how they will someday follow their husband's leadership. This training is being given, regardless of whether the wife is performing her task well or poorly, for modeling is always taking place. The children are observing the behavior of their mother, and they will emulate her when they begin their own family.

The Biblical Responsibility of Children

Husbands are commanded by God to lead, wives demonstrate great faith by following their leadership, and both are teaching their children by their examples whether good or bad. The Scripture specifically commands children to obey their parents, and this action takes faith, humility, and submission on their part. Ephesians 6:1 – "Children, obey your parents in the Lord, for this is right." Children are to obey their parents and God calls this "right." The word is actually translated as righteous in many translations, and it would seem to be the correct interpretation.

Colossians 3:20 – "Children, obey your parents in everything, for this pleases the Lord." Everything is an all-inclusive word.[62] As long as children are living under their parents' authority, they are always to be obedient in all ways at all times. Of course, this does not mean that the child is to perform sinful acts, or remain in a situation of abuse. However, in the normal course of a Christian home, with dad and mom attempting to follow God, children have one primary responsibility – to obey.

Even in homes where one, or both of the parents are not a Christian, the child can continue to learn a great many lessons if their heart remains submissive and open to God's instruction. God does not qualify the statement in either of the above verses limiting obedience to only godly parents. Parents can properly train, teach, and role model, but the duty of the child is to receive and implement what is being presented with a right attitude.

God makes a point of recording this concept in the Law. Paul in Ephesians 6:2 quotes Exodus 20:20 – "Honor your father and mother" (this is the first commandment with a promise). The first four of the Ten Commandments deal with the vertical relationship between God and humans. Commandment number five is the one Paul is sharing with the children, and as he mentions, is the only one with a promise. The promise is not necessarily guaranteeing that the individual child will live a long life, but that the people of God will prosper, and stay in the land of Promise, if they honor their parents. This commandment is not restricted to children. It was most likely directed to adults when given, for many of the commandments following this one

---

[62]. Vine, *An Expository Dictionary of New Testament Words*, 47. Pas - often translated as "all."

are broken primarily by adults. In short, God expects children to honor their parents regardless of age.

Children must be willing to humble themselves, and accept their parents' teaching and authority. God thought this process up and has given specific responsibilities to all involved in the family structure. The challenge to remain under authority becomes particularly difficult for children as they enter their adolescent years. However, true Christianity should be evident, and be making a difference in teenagers' lives, as well as the parents' lives. There are no Scriptures that clearly state that children are free to be out from under their parents' authority when they reach some arbitrary age like eighteen or twenty-one. The break appears to happen when the child leaves the home regardless of age.

The Non-Traditional Home

The discussion in this chapter has primarily dealt with a traditional, functioning family that includes a husband, wife, and one or more children that are all attempting to function as Christians. The realities of our day include families that do not match this description. Multiple divorces by one or both of the parental team tend to cloud the lines of love and loyalty. Stepbrothers and half-sisters present further problems for parents desiring acceptance from these children and not necessarily a leadership role. "You are not my real mother," or "You love your own children more than mine," are typical statements endured.

Dysfunctional homes due to alcohol, drugs, and mental issues, are becoming common in the current society. Often parents that are under the influence of these substances turn abusive or at least neglectful of their children or stepchildren.

Next, there are Christian spouses married to unbelievers, or even those of a competing faith, and this creates tension in the home regarding the religious training of the children, or the acceptable standards within the home.

Single-parent homes are rapidly becoming as numerous as those of two-parent homes are. The single parent struggles to be both mother and father to their children often while attempting to support the family financially, thus limiting the parental involvement.

The difficulties encountered in these homes, simply underline the importance of the breakdown of the family, and its devastating effect on the next generation. It is beyond the scope of this book to attempt to delve into the results of these tragedies, but even in these broken situations, the Scripture gives insight and patterns on how these types of homes should function.

The blended homes populated with half siblings and step relatives still can follow the Biblical guidelines addressed earlier. While not venturing into a discussion on divorce and remarriage, the Scriptures dealing with love, husband and wife relationships, and children honoring their parents, apply regardless of how many marriages each spouse may have had before the current one.

The husband, who is married to a non-believing spouse, can find comfort from reading Hosea for example. Hosea was commanded by God to marry an immoral woman, yet love her, and redeem her, even after repeated failures. It is hoped that the non-Christian spouse is not cheating on the husband as Hosea's wife did, but even if immorality is involved, there is still hope for reconciliation. The husband in such a case still has to attempt to love his wife as Christ loved the church, and he still has to train his children according to the Ephesians passage discussed earlier.

The wife married to a non-Christian can find comfort from Paul's instruction in 1 Corinthians 7, and perhaps even lead him to the Lord, without preaching to him. The wife still needs to be wise in her words, and learn how to exercise even greater faith by trusting God to lead through her unsaved husband.

Christian children of parents, who are not believers, still must obey them, and attempt to find something to honor in them according to God's commandment. Difficult home situations hinder the transference of faith from one generation to the next, but it does not alter the individual underlying responsibilities of each family member as previously revealed in the Scripture.

Before moving on, let me summarize some key points. Fathers must love and lead by being servants. Mothers must watch their words to assure that life is being spoken, and not death. Children are commanded to obey and honor their parents in everything. When these roles are followed, the transference of faith from one generation to the next has a significantly better chance of taking place.

We briefly mentioned the struggles of the non-traditional home. While there are difficult issues to grapple with in these homes, the Bible does offer hope and specific instruction for those living in them. In addition, the underlying roles of each family member remain the same regardless of the problems presented by the situation.

Next Stop:

Throughout the material presented so far, there has been no specific mention of the organized religious institution's role in the faith transference process. Families gathered together for worship, sacrifices, and participation in organized feasts, but little has been revealed as to the responsibility of the organized religious community. This was evident in the Old, and well as the New Testament.

While the Biblical emphasis is on the family's responsibility, the Church does play a role in the faith transference process as well.

The next chapter will begin to examine the role of the organized Church on the transference of faith into the next generation.

7 THE ROLE OF THE CHURCH

It is clear that the Scripture presents a significant amount of instruction directed to parents and children in their various roles and responsibilities. The family model is reflected throughout both Testaments demonstrating the blessings of success, and the heartache of failure. It has been noted that when fathers are active and involved, a positive result can occur, such as in the cases of the Rechabites and Philip. Conversely, parental failures such as Eli and Solomon reaped a different outcome. The absence of the organized religious institution's participation in these stories, either the Temple service of the Old Testament, or the Church of the New, is striking. This begs the question of what was, or perhaps more important, is, the role of the Church in the challenge of impartation of faith into the next generation. As was outlined in the initial chapters, the organized Church is heavily invested in reaching the young, implying that She believes there is a role to be played.

While there are limited passages dedicated to the organized church's direct role, several verses can be examined in the New Testament in an attempt to glean trends or patterns concerning children.

Children in the Early Church

Jesus always seemed to welcome children into His presence when He walked the earth. When Jesus performed the feeding of the 5,000 and 4,000, children are specifically mentioned as being present in the gatherings. (Matthew 14:21, 15:38) In Matthew 19:13-14 parents were bringing their children to Jesus to be blessed, and the disciples attempted to dissuade them. For their efforts, the disciples were rebuked by Jesus, "Let the little children come to me and do not hinder them, for to such belongs the kingdom of heaven." In Matthew 21:15 children are in and around the temple crying out:

> But when the chief priests and the scribes saw the wonderful things that he did, and the children crying out in the temple, "Hosanna to the Son of David!" they were indignant...

During this Passover celebration, the children were obviously part of the religious activities. There is no hint in the Gospel record of children or youth being separated from their parents in any of the gatherings around Jesus and His ministry. Jesus embraced children and even used them as illustrations and challenges to His disciples covering subjects that ranged from pride to faith.

> Acts 2:39 –"For the promise is for you and for your children and for all who are far off, everyone whom the Lord our God calls to himself."

As Peter was explaining the outpouring of the Holy Spirit, he mentioned that this promise is for all, including the children. Without venturing into the theology surrounding the outpouring of the Holy Spirit, the children were included in the promise of the Holy Spirit right alongside the adults. The reference may simply pertain to future generations but based on other New Testament passages about entire households being saved, perhaps not. In addition, who are those that "are far off" if they are not future believers? Perhaps this is a reference to future Gentile believers, or those in the Diaspora, but then again, it may also be referring to future generations. No matter whom Peter may have been referring to when he said, "those who are far off," John Gill believed that the parents mentioned were greatly concerned for their children's welfare. Many such commentators believed that this crowd had probably been the same ones that had called down curses on their children's head during their cries for Jesus' crucifixion.[63] Regardless of whom those are that "are far off," the parents were concerned for their children's survival, and the Holy Spirit was promised to all.

Unfortunately, there are recorded in Scripture very few glimpses into what the early Church services must have been like. It is revealed from reading Acts 2:42-47, that the Church met often in houses to eat and pray together, the temple for prayer and worship, and that they were devoted to the apostles' teaching. Since the Scripture does not address the issue, logically it can only be assumed that the entire family was present during most of these events. This assumption is not a wild one, but based on rational deduction. Families would not have been normally separated in Jewish culture, unless in the synagogue meeting, where the men and women were isolated. Even in the synagogue, the children would have been with their mothers, and not in the care of someone else. In addition, the Scripture mentions entire households coming to Christ in Acts 16:15, 34, with no distinction being made to gender or age.

After thirty years or more, the Scripture provides another glimpse into church life in Paul's letters to the Corinthians. The

---

[63]". Acts," in *The New John Gill's Exposition of The Entire Bible* (Paris AR: The Baptist Standard Bearer, 1999).

break with the synagogue was mostly complete by this time, and the Christian church was meeting in a new fashion. In 1 Corinthians 11 Paul addresses, the unruly eating of the Lord's Supper, and in chapter 14 he addresses order in the assembly between men and women.

In Paul's writings to this Church, there is a noticeable absence of any instructions dealing with childcare, child teaching, youth instruction, schools, classes, or any age-segregated issues. However, Paul gives specific instructions for widows, singles, husbands, wives, children, lawsuits, communion, elders, sexual temptation, spiritual gifts and warfare, the restoration of someone in sin, the place, and purpose of Israel, and a host of other issues. It is therefore not unreasonable to assume that if Paul wanted to give a pattern for ministry to children and youth, he could have found an opportunity to do so somewhere in his letters

Since many of Paul's letters were circulated among the churches, the assumption can be readily made that the role of the family members would have been studied and preached by the teaching elders. From this deduction, at least one of the roles of the Church in the impartation of faith to the next generation would have been the teaching of proper family roles.

Before leaving the writings of Paul, there is one more passage to consider, Ephesians 4:11-12:

> And he gave the apostles, the prophets, the evangelists, the pastors and teachers, to equip the saints for the work of ministry, for building up the body of Christ...

One of the clearly defined duties of the pastor is to equip the saints for ministry, and to build up the body of Christ. David Guzik explains that the word, "equip" means, "to be put right, the idea of mending a net, or fixing a broken bone.[64]" Using this

---

[64]. David Guzik's Commentary, "Ephesians," StudyLight.org,

understanding, one of a pastor's primary duties should include fixing broken families, of which our current churches abound.

Another New Testament author, John the beloved, provides specific instructions to various age groups in 1 John 2:12-14. In this lengthy passage, the aged apostle addresses, "little children" "fathers" "children" and "young men." It is difficult to discern exactly what age distinctions John had in mind when he wrote these instructions, since most of his readers would be substantially younger than he was. Perhaps John was attempting to deal with the way different age groups learn, or perhaps varying capacitates in processing information. Whatever he had in mind, he did emphasize some difference between the age groups, and that points to reality of all of the ages being together when this letter was read, not separated.

Church References in the New Testament

Performing any type of search, via either paper or electronic Biblical concordance, will reveal very few further insights as to *how* the early Church functioned. There are references to churches that met in homes, and letters addressed to churches in cities, but we are provided with little tangible insight on how to conduct "church." The New Testament contains significant revelations of doctrine, theology, and how to walk out the Commandments in a relational setting, but very few specific instructions on how to organize and operate the local Church. Therefore, it is difficult to establish the proper pattern (or only pattern) for an effective New Testament church. Any research that is limited to the Scripture will be hard pressed to ascertain with exactness what took place concerning specifics in a large number of arenas, including church government, role of women, trans-local authority, and age-integration or segregation.

---

http://www.studylight.org/com/guz/view (accessed September 25, 2008).

What *is* revealed in the New Testament is part of what the early Church did together, including praying, fellowshipping, and studying the apostles' teaching. What is not revealed is *how* they did these things. In addition, it is recorded that the Church met in homes, the temple, by rivers, and anywhere two or more were gathered. The New Testament writings provide specific instructions for each member of the family regarding the walking out their faith, but again, a total lack of how they did what was commanded. Paul required an elder to have a believing, disciplined family in order to be qualified for leadership, so obviously it was important how the family functioned.

It is not recorded anywhere if there were other classes presented, seminars given, retreats, or age-segregated meetings, for the Scripture is silent on these topics. It is clear that children were often present when Jesus, Peter, and Paul spoke. One young man fell out of a window when Paul spoke (Acts 20) and the Scripture mentions entire households being baptized. What is not recorded is if there were times when the children and young people were isolated into age-segregated groups for entertainment or instruction.

What is left then is to make judgments based on patterns, culture, and inferences, which will take place in the chapter analyzing the results of my research. The Scripture is strangely silent on this topic. Perhaps because it was a common understanding that parents would be responsible for the training of their children, and the church was not expected to replace or compete for that role, but to supplement it.

Historical Considerations Outside of the Biblical Record

What I have covered so far has primarily focused on the Biblical record. However, there is benefit in looking briefly at three of the Church's greatest statesmen and attempting to glean what they believed about the role of the family and Church regarding faith impartation. Augustine, Luther, and Jonathan Edwards all wrote on this topic, and each one envisioned a partnership between the parents and the church. Their writings will not be examined in detail, but quotes from each man will reveal some of what they believed.

One point to consider is that each of these men wrote long before any modern or post-modern mindset had infiltrated the Church. Each of these men would envision the role of the Church as that of instructing young people primarily in doctrine and creed, and never would have embraced such methods as discussed in chapter two of this book. A seriousness of study would have enveloped any endeavor of the Church to teach children as each of these men lived long before adolescent culture and rebellion became acceptable as normal.

Augustine addressed parenting and the role of the church in his famous *Confession:*

> Do my job in your own homes. A bishop is called such because he supervises, because he has to watch over those in his care. So everyone of you in his own house, if he is the head of the household, has the task of *bishoping*, of supervising, how his people believe, seeing that none of them drift into heresy, not his wife, nor his son, nor his daughter, nor even his slave, because he was bought for such a high price .

> Don't disdain the least of your people, keep a very
> watchful eye over the welfare and salvation of all your
> household.[65]

Bishops were in a position of authority and were required to
keep a watchful eye over their congregations. Augustine applies
this principle to fathers and challenges them to be in authority
over their home, making sure that each member of the home is a
believer and is not drifting into heresy. The father was challenged
to assure that his family was following the teachings of the
church. The comparison between being a bishop in the religious
order and the home is an excellent picture. Both the father and
the bishop are responsible for those under their direct charge.

Augustine was fond of long titles as demonstrated by the
following one in which he addresses the need for corporal
discipline in a school setting: *Of the Miseries and Ills to Which the
Human Race is Justly Exposed Through the First Sin, and from Which None
Can Be Delivered Save by Christ's Grace.*

> For what mean those multifarious threats which are used
> to restrain the folly of children? What mean pedagogues,
> masters, the birch, the strap, the cane, the schooling
> which Scripture says must be given a child, beating him
> on the sides lest he wax stubborn.[66]

---

[65] Augustine – *Confessions*
http://people.vanderbilt.edu/~james.p.burns/chroma/marriage
/martmar.html (accessed June 17, 2009)
[66] Augustine - Chapter 22.—Of the Miseries and Ills to Which
the Human Race is Justly Exposed Through the First Sin, and
from Which None Can Be Delivered Save by Christ's Grace.
http://www.ccel.org/ccel/schaff/npnf102.iv.XXII.22.html?high
light=children,school#highlight (accessed June 17, 2009)

Obviously, children were receiving schooling at the hands of those outside of the home. For generations it was common knowledge that if a child received a beating at school, they would often endure a second one at home, as the parents and church/school were partners in helping the child to develop. Augustine finishes this quote with his general view of youth and fallen man: "Inactivity, sloth, laziness, negligence, are vices which shun labor, since labor, though useful, is itself a punishment." According to Augustine, young and old alike deserved straps and canes in order to restrain the sinful nature enough in order that something of spiritual value could be imparted to them through their teachers!

Luther in his *Fourth Catechism* instructed children regarding the fifth commandment:

> We must, therefore impress it upon the young that they should regard their parents as in God's stead, and remember that however lowly, poor, frail, and queer they may be, nevertheless they are father and mother given them by God. They are not to be deprived of their honor because of their conduct or their failings.[67]

A catechism by definition is a systemic teaching, and many times, it is presented by the church to various population groups under its care. It is highly probable that Luther intended for children to memorize these teachings and quite likely that they would have received them in some type of church setting. The parents would have been expected to drill the children on the material throughout the week and then the children would be tested by the church leaders sometime later.

------

[67] Luther - The large catechism The Fourth Commandment. http://www.ccel.org/ccel/luther/large_cat/files/large_catechism06.htm (accessed June 17, 2009)

For all authority flows and is propagated from the authority of parents. For where a father is unable alone to educate his [rebellious and irritable] child, he employs a schoolmaster to instruct him; if he be too weak, he enlists the aid of his friends and neighbors; if he departs this life, he delegates and confers his authority and government upon others who are appointed for the purpose.

The quote above is later in the same catechism, and Luther states that fathers must teach their children and even employ schoolmasters and the government if they cannot accomplish the task through ignorance or death. If the child was rebellious and irritable, then the task could be delegated to a schoolmaster. The assumption being that the schoolmaster would be of sufficient character to break the undesired attitudes and behavior.

In *Table Talk*, Luther mentions young people that are headed for the ministry. The church and the parents both had a responsibility to teach the young people the Holy Scriptures and to train them for ministry. Once trained, the young person would not be out of line to present themselves as a candidate for service in any parish that might become vacant.

> Young people must be brought up to learn the Holy Scriptures; when such of them as know they are designed for the ministry present themselves and offer their service, upon a parish falling void, they do not intrude themselves.[68]

A final quote from Luther's *Treatise on Good Works* will show

---

[68] Luther – *Table Talk*
http://www.ccel.org/ccel/luther/tabletalk.v.xvii.html?highlight= children,teaching#highlight (accessed June 17, 2009)

what his standard was for those that taught in the organized school system.

> But spiritual authority should look to it, that adultery, unchastity, usury, gluttony, worldly show, excessive adornment, and such like open sin and shame might be most severely punished and corrected; and they should properly manage the endowments, monastic houses, parishes and schools, and earnestly maintain worship in them, provide for the young people, boys and girls, in schools and cloisters, with learned, pious men as teachers, that they might all be well trained, and so the older people give a good example and Christendom be filled and adorned with fine young people.[69]

Luther believed that schools were intended to be a place where worship and spiritual instruction took place. And, an environment in which true Christianity could be demonstrated by pious men as teachers. The goal stated is that this effort would produce the young people so well trained that Christendom could be filled with godly young people. A partnership between parents and the godly men of the church would be needed to accomplish this noble task.

Jonathan Edwards is the clearest of the three historical giants under consideration as to the role of the church regarding faith impartation. In a stark rebuke to fellow ministers in his *Works of Jonathan Edwards Volume Two: Examining the Lord's Day*, Edwards blasts the men for not being involved enough in overseeing their families in their churches. Edwards clearly states that the church has a direct responsibility for all the persons of the church, including the children. His specific charge is in dealing with the

---

[69] Luther - *Treatise on Good Works*
http://www.ccel.org/ccel/luther/good_works.vii.html?highlight
=school#highlight (accessed June 17, 2009)

administration of the ordinances of the church, and their neglect, but it is interesting that the children are mentioned as being under the authority of the church and the pastor.

> Are you not guilty of allowing yourselves in sin, in neglecting to do your part towards the removal of scandals from among us? All persons that are in the church, and the children of the church, are under the watch of the church; and it is one of those duties to which we are bound by the covenant which we either actually or virtually make, in uniting ourselves to a particular church, that we will watch over our brethren, and do our part to uphold the ordinances of God in their purity. This is the end of the institution of particular churches, viz. the maintaining of the ordinances of divine worship there, in the manner which God hath appointed.[70]

Edwards does not go entirely over to the extreme that the church should do everything in the instructing process of the children, but certainly that the church had a responsibility to assure that the children of its members were genuine believers. The following quote is taken also from his second volume of works but it is found in a section entitled; *Self-examination respecting the families to which we belong.*

> Whether you do not live in sin, by living in the *neglect of instructing* them. Do you not wholly neglect the duty of instructing your children and servants? or if you do not wholly neglect it, yet do you not afford them so little instruction, and are you not so unsteady, and do you not

---

[70] Works of Jonathan Edwards Volume Two: Examining the Lord's Day
http://www.ccel.org/ccel/edwards/works2.vi.v.v.html?highlight
=church,instructing,children#highlight (accessed June 17, 2009)

take so little pains in it, that you live in a sinful neglect? Do you take pains in any measure proportionate to the importance of the matter? You cannot but own that it is a matter of vast importance, that your children be fitted for death, and saved from hell; and that all possible care be taken that it be done speedily; for you know not how soon your children may die. Are you as careful about the welfare of their souls as you are of their bodies? Do you labour as much that they may have eternal life, as you do to provide estates for them to live on in this world?[71]

This rebuke strikes directly to heart of the father that is more concerned with providing an estate for his child, than for making sure the child is ready for his heavenly estate. Failure to instruct their children in eternal matters was equated with "sinful neglect."

This brief section dealing with Augustine, Luther, and Edwards demonstrates that down through the ages there was a partnership between the church and home with the unified goal of producing godly young people. While details may be sketchy, it is obvious that various methods and models have been used in this effort. It is apparent that parents would send their children to the church to be instructed in doctrine, creeds, and catechism, and the church would expect the parents to reinforce the church's message during the time between services. By this partnership, both realms of authority would be strengthened.

The Family-Integrated Church Movement

Many churches and leaders across the country are attempting

---

[71] Works of Jonathan Edwards Volume Two; Self-examination respecting the families to which we belong. http://www.ccel.org/ccel/edwards/works2.vi.v.ix.html (accessed June 18, 2009)

to change the common format of the local church referenced in chapter two, to a more age-integrated model. These leaders are doing so because they believe the absence of age-segregated instruction in the Scripture allows them to attempt an entirely different approach to the local church. Some, though not all, believe this model is actually the Biblically accurate one. Since we do not have the entire historical record recorded for us in Scripture, it would not be prudent to go that far. In addition, the Scripture is silent on many of these topics, as has already been pointed out, so it is difficult to be adamant.

Specifically in light of the goal of this book, the family-integrated church movement is experiencing the inverse ratio of young people rejecting their parent's faith compared to the age-segregated model. The statistics in chapter one revealed a 70-90% rejection rate for churched young people when they leave High School. From personal observation, as well as peer discussions with other pastors of family-integrated churches, the rate of rejection in the family-integrated movement would be substantially less. In fact, a study quoted in the next chapter reveals almost an exact inverse ratio for those children that were home educated, and, in most family-integrated churches, the vast majority of members will home educate their children.

This new movement is relatively young and there are few formal studies being attempted yet to effectively ascertain with certainness that the results of this movement are different than those reflected in chapter one. However, nearly twenty year observation, the results to date offer encouragement. While there are young people that will reject their families' teachings and value system upon reaching college age, the numbers have been substantially less than those raised in the currently popular model have.

Hope Family Fellowship began in December 1993 and is currently one of the oldest and largest churches in the family-integrated movement. The church has over 350 active participants, with some traveling over an hour to attend the weekly services. Moreover, the national landscape is changing rapidly with new works springing up all over the country. In recent years, at least three national groups have formed that are attempting to help promote and mentor these type churches. There are most likely others that are not as visible or well known.

Vision Forum is a well-respected group that includes a national database of hundreds of family-integrated churches entitled, "The National Center for Family-Integrated Churches.[72]" The Council for Family-Integrated Churches represents a growing group of churches with its membership[73] from coast to coast. Recently, Dr. Voddie Baucham received a significant amount of national airtime on many radio programs promoting this new movement. In addition, Dr. Baucham has begun to build a network of like-minded churches that is growing very rapidly.[74] These three groups have hundreds of member churches, and many of these works are experiencing an explosive growth pattern. Initial surveys from these groups indicate a high percentage of faith transference taking place with little rejection of the parent's faith.

Several realities make a family-integrated church different from all of the other churches that advertise themselves as "family churches." These are distinctions, which are unrelated to denominational structure, or even the typical groupings along

---

[72]. Doug Phillips, "Vision Forum Ministries," September, 2008, The National Centering for Family-integrated Churches, http://www.visionforumministries.org (accessed September 25, 2008).

[73]. The Council for Family-Integrated Churches "C4FIC," September, 2012, http://www.C4FIC.org (accessed September 25, 2012).

[74]. GFBC, "Alliance for Church & Family Reformation," September, 2008, GFBC, http://www.gracefamilybaptist.net (accessed September 25, 2008).

various theological viewpoints. The family-integrated church model is being used in reformed and non-reformed works, charismatic, and non-charismatic, conservative traditional, and the more modern counterparts. The practical workings of this model will be explained in the next chapter.

A comment heard often is, "This is the first church that is reinforcing my views from the pulpit." And, "I don't have to protect my children from the church here." This is not to say that churches that maintain a family-segregated culture are wrong or wicked, only that what these particular families were looking for, was not available to them in the age-segregated model. The typical people that are drawn to the family-integrated church model are desirous of being the major influence in their children's lives. Many times in a traditional church, young people are encouraged to follow a youth leader or Sunday school teacher that may or may not have the same value system of the parents. In addition, the pastor may or may not reinforce the family-integrated perspective that these families are seeking, so parents are concerned that the children are receiving a mixed message from the churches leadership.

Many at the family-integrated church have larger than normal families, and some have suffered insulting comments from their previous churches. "Don't you know what causes that many children?" Or, "Stay away from the drinking fountain." "Are you guys Catholic or something, why in the world would you want six (or eight or twelve) kids?" Presumably, most of the comments are meant to be funny, but in a society where children are not valued as highly as they once were, they often are taken as insulting to a family that desires to have twelve or more children.

To illustrate the differences further consider a common story from families that have been asked to leave the sanctuary for keeping their children with them instead of sending them to the children's church or nursery. "The pastor doesn't like to have children making noise during the service," they are told. "Well our children don't make noise for we have trained them to sit quietly," the family replies. The usher continues, "We have an excellent children's church and nursery, would you please take your children there." The family replies, "We prefer to keep them with us." The usher gets more impatient and explains that the pastor simply does not want children in the church. Somewhere an elderly man has a coughing attack and several others drop hymnals making a loud noise, and eventually the family leaves the church.

Some families with older children have explained that they had a difficult time following the leadership in their church due to the role models being presented by the leader's lifestyle. Comments from the pulpit referencing TV shows or movies that the family found offensive or the clothing choices being made by the pastor's family were not supporting the more modest lifestyle chosen by these families, and it became increasing more difficult to explain to the children. "Why does elder so and so allow his children to dress that way and we can't?" Or, "The pastor thought that movie was funny, why are you and mom against it?" There are of course many acceptable ways to dress and to entertain ourselves, which are not clearly defined in the Scripture, but the struggling family feels out of place and looks to move on to another church that reflects its conservative viewpoints. The comments referenced above are merely reflective of people searching for a church that represented a more conservative choice, and the increasing difficulty of finding one. These type comments are not necessarily indicative of age-segregation versus age-integration; however, many in the family-integration movement will have a very conservative viewpoint of these issues.

As previously mentioned, most member families of this model will home educate their children for the same reasons as they attend a family-integrated church. These parents desire to observe and assure that their children are being taught what the parents desire, and not necessarily the church or private schools.

Most family-integrated churches would follow what is referred to by Penny Becker as, "The Family Cultural Model." In Ms. Becker's book, *Congregations in Conflict, Cultural Models of Local Religious Life;* the "family" model is summed up as follows: "The best summary is to say that their congregation fosters a general sense of well being, acceptance, and belonging.[75]" The number one comment family-integrated churches will hear from visiting families is that they finally feel like they have found a home, a family where they fit in and are no longer the weird ones! People of like-mind tend to gather. For the large family that is desirous of being the primary influence in their children's lives, the family-integrated church model has proved to be very popular.

Next Stop:

In the next chapter, we will begin to explore the age-segregated model and some of its major drawbacks. In addition, some respected leaders from previous generations chime in through their writings.

---

[75]Penny Edgell Becker, *Congregations in Conflict, Cultural Models of Local Religious Life* (New York, New York: Cambridge University Press, 1999), 82.

8 PROBLEMS WITH THE CURRENT MODEL

What has been presented so far paints a clear picture that the family is centric to God's plan and purposes. The overwhelming family emphasis in the Bible points to a specific plan and not a random act. God chose to have children born into a family structure instead of some other method that was open to Him. God directly charged the parents with the responsibility to teach, train, and restrain. While parents are free to delegate some of the training to whomever they wish, it is clear that God still holds the parents responsible for the instruction, and the ultimate behavior of their children. In the Old Testament patriarchal days, this extended into adulthood, as demonstrated by Eli and Samuel. From these and other Biblically historical narratives, it became clear that there were generational consequences to parental choices. Eli's failure to restrain his grown sons cost his family the priesthood. Conversely, Jonadab found in Jeremiah 35 will always have a descendant that follows the Lord.

The fact that God "thinks" and acts generationally is demonstrated in the following verses, Exodus 34:6-7:

> The LORD passed before him and proclaimed, "The LORD, the LORD, a God merciful and gracious, slow to anger, and abounding in steadfast love and faithfulness,

keeping steadfast love for thousands, forgiving iniquity and transgression and sin, but who will by no means clear the guilty, visiting the iniquity of the fathers on the children and the children's children, to the third and the fourth generation."

Isaiah 59:21 repeats this principle:

And as for me, this is my covenant with them," says the Lord: "My Spirit that is upon you, and my words that I have put in your mouth, shall not depart out of your mouth, or out of the mouth of your offspring, or out of the mouth of your children's offspring," says the Lord, "from this time forth and forevermore.

We will not develop these concepts in detail, but it is clear that God intended that there would be generational interaction and consequences between parents and children.

In the Old Testament, there are no clear references about the *specific role* that organized religion played in imparting faith to the next generation. The tabernacle and temple would have been central to Old Testament thinking and acting, but there are no direct verses explaining what that role was in the family's attempt to pass on the faith to their children.

Families assembled together, but little insight is given into what they actually did as families or individuals. Law was given which explained how to perform various worship oriented acts, but nothing to designate what role each family member played in the process. Ages are given for minimum service for priests and soldiers, and even the retirement age for those who served in the temple, but nothing as to whether children were part of the religious activities and what role they played if any.

A significant part of the Law was written to help a nation of former slaves learn basic human relationship skills. For four hundred years, the Children of Israel lived their lives roughly equivalent to that of a dog. In one day, this mass of humanity was released, and they needed instructions in some of the most basic social skills. Laws on how to treat each other, sexual laws, thievery laws, borrowing laws, and dozens of other practical commands helped to bring order to the mob. Nevertheless, even within this mass of laws, there was none that specifically addressed the training of children in any fashion that precluded or excluded the direct involvement of the parents.

Parents were instructed however, to make sure their children understood what God had done, and why. It was observed that the reading of the Law would take place at various times, and the family would gather including children, but there is no mention of any specific age-segregated activity. There are no references to any children's messages, youth groups, or any isolating of the family by age-segregation.

Some in the family-integrated arena seem to believe that there are two veiled references to youth groups in the Old Testament, but this is a stretch of basic hermeneutical principles. The first one is when Rehoboam listened to his peers (young men) instead of the older counselors in 1 Kings 12. The second one actually does contain a mention of forty-two youths, they, however, had a bad experience with two she-bears in 2 Kings 2. Other than these two questionable references, it is very difficult to find any mention of groups of children and youth. There was of course a "school of the prophets," but we know little of their ages, methodology, and even purpose.

In the New Testament, the pattern remained the same as the Old. There are no Scriptures explaining the *direct* role of the organized Church in imparting faith to the next generation. There are many verses specifically dealing with the individual family member's roles, but little revealed about the actual role of the church. From the verses considered previously, it is observable that children were typically part of the religious gatherings and probably participated in the events recorded. The Scripture also quotes Jesus' bidding the children to "come unto Him" and Peter stated that the Holy Spirit was going to be poured out upon the children some day. Clearly, salvation came to entire households, and the children were being fed alongside their parents at two of Jesus' miraculous feedings. Jesus even challenged His followers to become like children in their faith, so children were obviously part of the events recorded in the New Testament.

Paul addressed many specific issues of theology and ministry practice in his extensive writings, but there is almost a complete absence of any direct commands as to the role of the organized church regarding instructing children. There is the understanding in Scripture that everyone matures at various rates of spiritual growth, but little direct attention given to the specific role played by the Church in that process. Paul addressed the need for elder candidates to have their families under control and in order. Paul included disobedience in children in lists that included murder, and other heinous crimes, and as a sign of the last days. In addition, Paul explained in detail the roles of each family member including singles and widows. However, there is no mention or instructions given on *how* to deal with children and youth in the Church. In Timothy and Titus, the two letters specifically written to young men containing instructions on "setting things in order," would have been opportune places to include these breakdowns, however, they are omitted.

This book is not intended to prove or disprove whether age-segregation is an acceptable method, for clearly there are many acceptable means of teaching and attempting to pass on faith generationally. The goal of my book is to discover what the Bible presents as the roles of the family and the Church in the faith transference process. It is clear from the Scripture that the family is the *primary* means of generational faith transference. In addition, it is clear that the Church is to teach and equip family members to be successful in their role within the family, and to mature in their Christian walk.

The Scripture does not provide a complete picture of how families interacted with the religious institutions in either the Old or New Testament. The way the Bible is written provides significant gaps in the historical narratives leaving us with little day-to-day information. In addition, the New Testament is primarily a record of Jesus and His Church, and not a family training manual. We are giving highlights, illustrations, principles, and often not minute details, so dogmatic conclusions are difficult. One conclusion is clear in both Testaments; God intended for the family to be deeply involved in the process of faith transference between the generations, and for the organized religious community to assist them.

An Analysis of the Drawbacks of the Current Age-Segregated Model

Chris Schlect has pointed out some of the obvious dangers of peer groupings:

> When young people exclusively interact with one another and make their own rules, a "herd mentality" develops: they follow in the footsteps of one another rather than those of adults.[76]

Most of us are familiar with some of the "herd mentality" mindset. Clothing fads are an obvious one. While visiting in Hong Kong several years ago, it was apparent that thousands of women were wearing shoes with a very sharp pointed toe. In fact, they looked like elf shoes. Over the next couple of years,

---

[76]. Schlect, A Critique of Youth Ministries,"
http://www.soulcare.org/education/youth. (accessed September 19, 2008)

this style became "hot" in my city, and the stores were soon filled with these shoes. Shortly thereafter, the "herd" began wearing pointed shoes. The shoes, it was revealed, were uncomfortable and potentially hazardous, yet, many women wore them. Soon, they are nowhere to be seen. The same has been true with mini-skirts, Beatle boots, and many other items, each of which became "in" or "out" overnight. In the 1980's, a colorful, very expensive running shoe was "in." Everyone had to have one to be accepted and many families that could not afford the shoe, which cost over $100, still purchased the shoe. The typical Church age grouping and isolation of the young, does not provided for, nor typically allow the necessary parental supervision and input on such thinking. The Biblical pattern presented seems to imply that children should follow in their parents' example, not their peers.

Brandon Dauphinais observed,

> One of the hardest losses due to the modern age-segregated church is the deteriorating household structure. The modern system does not encourage unity in the households. Married couples go to one class, older men and women go to their men's and women's classes respectively, while "teens" go to their youth groups, and finally children wind up in their own personal peer classes. When this system is in place, it builds passive boundaries that separate the members in each household.[77]

---

[77]. Brandon Dauphinais, "The Age-Integrated Church," 2002, B. Dauphinais, http://www.utmost-way.com/theageintegratedchurcharticle.htm (accessed September 29, 2008).

"Passive boundaries" seem to add to the "generation gap" that our society embraced in the 1950's and 60's. Intergenerational relationships are discouraged by the artificial groupings of the age-segregated system. If each member of the family has an entirely different peer group, there remains little in the way of cross-pollination of ideas and wisdom, and it restricts the building of friendships across these artificial boundaries.

The reality is that very few will ever encounter a situation where a large amount of time is spent in age-segregated environments once the teenage years pass.

Lilian Katz, Ph.D. a professor of early childhood education at the University of Illinois, believes that "there are many potential benefits to both children and adults when children are mixed with others of different ages."[78] Katz, in the same article, also states that, "In mixed age groups, older children are encouraged and expected to help the younger ones. Younger children who are assisted by the older ones will do the same in their turn when they are seniors." Thus, the transference by example and words are passed on. Katz also addresses several other advantages gained by both groups, including social skills, communication competence, complex play enhancement, and more mature problem solving skills.

Another issue to consider is the downgrading of the material that is typically presented in the age-segregated environment. The curriculums used by children and youth ministry are often depleted of theology and other in-depth Bible doctrines to assure that what is present is easily absorbed. Rather than challenging the youth to step up to adulthood, the children are taught "watered-down" lessons. The parents are alleviated of the

[78]. Lilian Katz, "The Benefits of the Mix," November, 1998, Child Care Information Exchange, http://www.childcareexchange.com (accessed August 22, 2008).

responsibility of making sure that their children glean something of value from the sermon by the pastor, because they have had a Bible story acted out by puppets or by a skit of peers.

The "dummying down" of education in America is well documented.[79] It is not a stretch to think that this process has made inroads into the Church via the curriculums used in the age-segregated approach to ministry. Instead of the children and youth being taught to take notes and then ask questions of their parents, they are presented with their own array of materials geared to their age level. Debate may rage over how far down the materials are degraded, but by the nature of having age-segregated materials, the groups clearly are being presented with materials less weighty than the adults are grappling with. C. S. Lewis, expressing his outrage over this process, poetically states: "He may be hostile, but he cannot be critical; he does not know what is being discussed."[80] Lewis is stating that we have taken the challenge out of our education system by lowering the standards of acceptable comprehension to such a level that people may scream, but they simply are not educated enough to even understand the issues. In picturesque style, Lewis bemoans that we have created a generation of people that we expect greatness from, but have ill equipped them. The obvious connection is that when we isolate children and youth away from adult-level materials and discussions, we are cheating them out of potential wisdom and growth.

We provided juvenile materials and immature youth leaders to our young people, and then marvel at how childish they act. The typical antics described in chapter two of this research, fall way short of Paul's admonition to his young protégé Timothy in 1

---

[79]. Charlotte Thomson Iserbyt, "The Deliberate Dumbing Down of America," 2000, Charlotte Thomson Iserbyt, http://www.delberatedumbindown.com (accessed September 30, 2008).

[80]. Lewis, *The Abolition of Man*, 47.

Timothy 4:12 – "Let no one despise you for your youth, but set the believers an example in speech, in conduct, in love, in faith, in purity." The standards demanded by Luther and Edwards for godly, mature men to lead the youth in the instruction of doctrine, are mostly not being followed in our day.

David Wells, in one of his blistering critiques of the status of the Evangelical church, made this observation:

> The most we seem able to do is to take daily inventories of personal needs and then try to match up people, products, and opportunities with them. The irony is that this psychological hedonism, in which self is the arbiter of life, is self-destructive.[81]

The age-integrated approach seems to fit into the above description. The children and youth are matched up with appropriate programs and departments in order to satisfy a perceived need of being relevant to their age group. Wells continues his assault:

> The church should be known as a place where God is worshiped, where the Word of God is heard and practiced, and where life is thought about and given its most searching and serious analysis...The interest turns to how well appointed and organized the church is, what programs it has to offer, how many outings the youth group has organized, how convenient it is to attend, how good the nursery is.[82]

Children and youth, instead of being exposed to the adult-level preaching, worship, and interaction, are relegated to smaller same age groupings, and one has to wonder what is lost in this

---

[81]. David F. Wells, *God in The Wasteland; The Reality of Truth in a World of Fading Dreams* (Grand Rapids, MI: Eerdmans, 1994), 14.
[82]. Ibid., 85.

process.

Wells also touches the issue from the angle of attempting to supplant parents and the impact that this choice is making on parental authority:

> This coalition of parental surrogates, cobbled together in a blind attempt to preserve the social order, has ironically had the effect of further diminishing the remaining parental authority.[83]

One final quote from Wells attempts to deal with the "just because it is popular does not mean it is correct" mindset that has entered into the Church. Large crowds, big staffs and buildings, do not necessarily equal correct orthodoxy or orthopraxy:

> It may be that it is only our enthusiasm for pragmatism- our assumption that only the consequences of an idea reveal whether it is true or false-that incline us to think that anything that succeeds in the marketplace must, in the nature of the case, be true and virtuous.[84]

Large numbers of participants, and even generally accepted agreement on a model, does not necessarily guarantee that it is a Biblical one. The majority opinion is not always the correct one.

---

[83]. Ibid.. 217.
[84]. Ibid.. 68.

Age-Segregation is Not a Biblically Mandated Module

Most of us would consider the Bible as the standard of all truth. If the Scripture were approached without any preconceived notions, we would never arrive on our own at some of the currently accepted conclusions on how to conduct ministry, and how properly to support the raising of a Christian family. For example, children becoming adults and independent at age eighteen, departmental ministry including youth groups and children's ministry, dating, generation gap, different music standards between parents and children, entertainment-oriented church, and a host of other concepts. None of these concepts is presented within the pages of Scripture, and therefore all of them have been added to the Biblical model from outside. That does not necessarily invalidate them, but if we were searching for what the Scriptures reveal or models, these would have to be seriously questioned.

Hinted at in the quotes from Wells is the premise that the Church has adopted a worldview that is primarily secular and not Biblical. In fact, reading Wells' books, he makes it abundantly clear that he believes that the Church has become capitalistic or market driven, in nature. In addition, the need to be relevant to as many people as possible seems to have crept into the current philosophy of ministry. For the last fifty years at least, age-segregation away from the parents has been the popular way to accomplish the goal of instructing young people.

Accepting the premise that children and youth need to be isolated and age grouped, the Church has tailored its ministry approach to accomplish the task. Ministries, publishers, and nationwide organizations have sprung up to meet this demand. Leaders are trained, degrees are offered, and supplies are produced, to reach this age-segregated demographic.

Parents are told that they need to be able to listen to the messages without distraction, so the Church provides quality programs for their children to allow the parents to concentrate. The Church has made it easy for the parents to delegate away their responsibility to teach and train their children in spiritual matters. The programs are so completely ingrained in the minds of almost everyone, that to think of not having them, paints a picture of need. The emphasis is on fine-tuning the technique of age-segregation, instead of ever questioning the underlying assumption of their validly. What is accomplish then is the young people, from nursery to high school, are separated from their parents in all Church related matters, thus promoting little spiritual communication between the generations.

Other Scholars' Viewpoints

John Calvin believed in infant baptism and offered no hint of age-segregation in his extensive writings. Infants were included in the life of the church, and as such, were candidates to receive forgiveness and baptism. A discussion of whether infant baptism is an acceptable practice is not the point, but simply that Calvin believed that children were part of the Church and were therefore not isolated into some separate grouping.

> The communicants or partakers are adults, after making a confession of their faith, and likewise infants; for baptism came in the place of circumcision, and in both the mystery, promise, use, and efficacy, are the same. Forgiveness of sins also belongs to infants, and therefore it is likewise a sign of this forgiveness.[85]

---

[85]. John Calvin, "Aphorisms," in *Institutes of the Christian Religion*, trans. Hevry Beveridge (Grand Rapids, MI: Eerdmans Publishing, 1997), 687.

Charles Hodge reflected upon the duty of fathers to instruct their children, and if they chose to delegate this away, they remained responsible to assure that the institution chosen will honor "these divine prescriptions."

> Train up a child in the way he should go; and he will not depart from it." (Proverbs 22:6) Fathers bring up your children "in the nurture and admonition of the Lord." (Ephesians 6:4) These are not ceremonial or obsolete laws. They bind the consciences of men just as much as the command, "Thou shall not steal.[86]

J. Rodman Williams writes,

> Children who are raised in godly homes and from their earliest days are trained in the faith find their later church experience all the more meaningful. Christian parents, not church pastors and teachers, have the primary responsibly...All in all, the home must be the primary center of Christian nurture and teaching.[87]

Children who experience the reality of Christ in the home do not have the luxury of finger pointing about hypocrisy in their parents. Parents have the primary responsibility to present the power of the Gospel to their children by demonstrating how it has changed their own lives. There is a place for the Church teachings to reinforce what the parents are attempting to impart to their children; they should however, be in conjunction with, not competing with, what the ones primarily responsible are

---

[86]. Charles Hodge, *Systematic Theology Volume III*, Fourth ed. (Peabody, MA: Hendrickson Publishers, 2008), 355.

[87]. J. Rodman Williams, *Renewal Theology - The Church, the Kingdom, and Last Things* (Grand Rapids, MI: Zondervan Publishing House, 1992), 116.

attempting to accomplish.

In 1970 a little book entitled, *The Christian Family* was penned by Larry Christenson. This book has far surpassed several million copies sold. This is an older book but its truths are still very relevant today. Notice what Christenson says about worship.

> Jesus' presence in the family comes to its sharpest focus as the family gathers in His presence to worship. For worship is communion with God par excellence. In worship we gather in His presence; we assemble under His Lordship; we reach out to receive His grace; we listen to His Word; we submit ourselves to His will.[88]

Most Evangelicals would readily agree with Christenson's understanding of the worship service. During this time, we expect to sing, pray, and hear the Word of God expounded. This is an excellent time for children of all ages to experience the presence of God. If they are too young to understand what is going on, they still can glean a great deal from simply watching their parents. An attentive father, a note-taking mother, or older sibling, will speak volumes to a younger child as to the importance of the worship service. A pattern of being in God's house, together as a family unit, imprints a positive picture on young minds. It is logical that if the segregating of the family creates disunity, herd mentality, and builds passive boundaries, as mentioned in earlier chapters of this book, the uniting of the family should encourage the exact opposite of these negatives.

Like Augustine, Luther, and Edwards mentioned earlier, these scholars would not be against the organized church being involved in instructing children and youth. In fact, the drilling of catechism, Bible memorization, and in-depth instruction of the church Creeds would be strongly endorsed. However, like

---

[88]. Larry Christenson, *The Christian Family* (Minneapolis, MN: Bethany Fellowship, 1970), 166.

Calvin, Hodge, and Rodman, the early church leaders would desire for the parents to be engaged as the *primary* instructors of their own children.

Some Appropriate Age-Segregation Applications

The bulk of this book has led to the conclusion that family-integration is the normal Biblical pattern. However, there are times when age-segregation is appropriate and beneficial. The ages of children needs to be considered when discussing sensitive matters, like sexual behavior, or other marriage issues, for example. Conducting a sexual oriented teaching may not be appropriate for children of all ages. There are times when older children need to be grouped to discuss issues that younger children simply cannot relate to or even need to be exposed to yet. On other occasions, men and women need to gather exclusively to discuss topics that are not appropriate for a mixed gender group. However, even in these groups, it is not necessary to have strict age-segregation. Older women are charged by Paul to teach the younger ones, and older men are encouraged to be examples (Titus 2) to the younger brothers.

Some would argue for a singles ministry or college age grouping, but again, the principle is not found in Scripture. In the Old Testament the children often lived with their parents even after marriage, and in the New, we already mentioned Philip and his four grown daughters still living at home. In fact, Psalm 68:6 states, "God sets the lonely in families." Unmarried adults can have an effective ministry serving others, being role models for the younger, and being wholly devoted to the Lord. Isolating the single adults from the Church Body potentially hinders the transference of a positive example from one generation to another.

Ministries that focus on reaching the lost, or assisting youth from broken homes, are needed and they can serve a valuable purpose. However even in this endeavor it seems that if the young people that are grouped together and discipled, are then placed in functioning families, the retention rate of their faith would be significantly higher. There are times when the home is in such disarray that the Church needs to provide help and ministry that the parents are incapable of giving. However, again, it would seem more in line with the Biblical pattern to have the struggling young person attached to an older man or woman for guidance and comfort, instead of simply being grouped with peers. There are possibly other acceptable reasons for age-segregation; however, in any of them it would be closer to the Biblical example if parental involvement could be incorporated.

A Disclaimer of Sorts:

This book has attempted to examine the roles of parents and the organized Church in passing on faith to the next generation. The method was to present Biblical characters, comments from others, both well known, and not, and to mix in personal experiences and views. While the book was not intended to be a critique on children and youth ministry, these were naturally considered in comparison to the Biblical record. The discussion of any topic is always limited in its scope and cannot possibly cover all of the issues involved. Generalities and stereotypical examples sometimes are used to illustrate points. Like polling data, these techniques can provide a picture or a potential outcome, but it is indeed only seen through a glass darkly.

The methods used were searching for general patterns from Scripture and therein is one of the limits. To every general pattern, there are exceptions. My points confirm, that the family is centric and the first and best means of impartation of faith into the next generation. However, that does not necessarily mean that it is the *only* means acceptable. In addition, that does not mean that there are not other methods experiencing success. The statistics quoted in chapter one allow for there to be at least ten percent success and in some cases, thirty percent. Naturally, statistics as the ones used in chapter one are based on averages and these can be misleading. Averages include highs and lows and there are many successful age-segregated ministries that are not experiencing the low end of the studies referenced. Of course, that also means that there are ministries that are experiencing very high rates of failure.

My personal experiences relayed in this book have been limited to mostly white, middle class churches and youth oriented gatherings. Churches in the inner city face a very different set of challenges than the ones that I have experienced. With the rapid deterioration of the family, it is difficult to deal with the deluge of single-family homes, and unsupervised children. The Church may provide the only male role model for countless young people in such cases. Even dealing with this reality however, would not change the fact that the family model provides the one closest to the Scriptural model, and is the best opportunity for these challenging circumstances. However, it may not be possible in such situations to have enough families to assist, and therefore the Church must fulfill the role of surrogate parents.

It is beyond what I was trying to accomplish to develop the historical precedence and practices of the age-segregated model that are *outside* of the Biblical record. The point of this research is to determine if there is a Biblical pattern unveiled *within* the Scripture for the transference of faith from one generation to the next. Any generalized statement forbidding age-segregation is shortsighted for Sunday Schools and other age-segregated tools have been part of the Church for a long time. In addition, the absence of mention in Scripture does not disqualify usage for the currently accepted and prevalent age-segregated model.
On the other hand, neither does it endorse it.

The age-segregated model does have many attractive features

and these probably account for its current dominance in the Church. Moreover, as previously stated, there are times when age-segregation is necessary or preferred. Some advantages include: it is far less time consuming, and much easier to delegate the training of children to someone else. In the case of educational choices, the idea of a professional interacting with our children has a certain attraction, and greatly reduces our concerns about sending them off for large parts of the day. Committing the spiritual training into the hands of professionally trained children, youth workers, and pastors, also fits this understanding. Many parents are very eager to delegate the training of their children to those perceived as more qualified. While this book has focused on the Biblical record and pattern, that does not mean that there are not positives to the currently accepted method of age-segregation.

Finally, no two families are alike. It is impossible to ascertain a "normal" pattern of what Christianity looks like in a home or, for that matter, what a functioning home even is. The full impact on the next generation of the parents' relationship, communication skills, and their own personal problems, is impossible to grasp. Individual personalities as well, must play a role in this process of faith transference. Sibling relationships within the family and extended family must also play some role in the process. The influence of TV, internet, and mass media also presents challenges in parenting and faith impartation. Each of the above issues presents problems to generalized statements for they would surely distort, or at least influence, the outcome. What we are left with is the fact that each human is a unique person that is influenced by a great number of factors. These factors bear directly on decisions and choices that are made, including adopting or rejecting a parent's faith position.

In addition to the above, each child, as they enter adulthood, will have to face and either succumb to or overcome temptation.

The choices made will have a direct impact on how long or how deeply, a child maintains their parents' faith.

The pattern presented in the Scripture would lead to the conclusion that the age-integrated model is a more Biblical model than the age-segregated one, but the sheer number of potential influences in a young person's life, still affects the ultimate outcome of the process. This reality makes it harder to be dogmatic, but it does not change the findings of the research.

Next Stop:

In chapter nine, we will look at the family-integrated church model in detail. After explaining how the typical family-integrated church functions, we will move into an evaluation of the pastor's changing role in this ministry model.

9 THE FAMILY-INTEGRATED CHURCH

The implications of what has been presented so far, despite its aforementioned holes, should cause some serious consideration and introspection regarding the age-segregated Church model. If the studies reported in chapter one are true, and there certainly is no reason to doubt them, then the Church must seriously be open to pondering the reasons for the mass rejection of faith by the next generation. In addition, if the inverse ratio statistics documented by Dr. Ray in the final section of this book are accurate, and again, there is little reason to doubt them, the implications are staggering. In the first data presented, somewhere between 70-90% of young people are rejecting their parents' faith when they leave the home after High School, whereas in Dr. Ray's studies, 94% are not rejecting it. These results should not be ignored.

The Primary Philosophical Issue

Near the center of the two competing views rests a philosophical mindset. The issue grapples with *who* has the primary role and responsibility for the impartation of faith into the next generation.

While both groups would readily agree with these statements from Mark DeVries, their application would vary widely;

> "Really, the core identity of all churches should be to pass on their faith to the next generation and youth ministry is an essential to the future of a church."[89]

The philosophical battle between age-segregated and age-integrated will rage within the application of this sentence, and will primarily focus on *who* is responsible for that youth ministry, and how that ministry should be accomplished.

An article written by James Hampton and Mark Hayse, both highly sought after youth ministry professionals, highlights the philosophical differences clearly. "Family ministry, as it's commonly understood and practiced, may not be the best way to do youth ministry."[90] "Family ministry" referenced in the article, is understood in light of the commonly accepted framework of age-segregation, yet an attempt is made to reach each member of the family by intermingling the groups in some gatherings. Hampton and Hayse statement is based in part of a book written by Dr. Diana Garland;

> The typical family unit (father, mother, children), often referred to as the "nuclear" or "domestic" family, is what most people think of when we discuss family ministry. However, as Dr. Diana Garland, who has written several books on family ministry, has pointed out, a major

[89] Mark DeVries, "Youth Ministry 101" 2007, Youth Ministry.Com, www.youthministry.com/?q=node/5499 (accessed March 31, 2009)

[90] James Hampton, Mark Hayse, "A Different View of Family Ministry" 2009, Youth Specialties, http://www.youthspecialties.com/freeresources/articles/family/different_view.php (accessed March 31, 2009)

problem with using this type of definition is that the Bible, the church's statement of values, offers little support for defining a strong nuclear family as the goal of Christian relationships.

Shifting away from the nuclear family as preeminent towards the family of faith being central, does move the discussion to a different plane as emphasized in the next quote;

> In his book *Ties That Stress*, psychologist David Elkind even insists that the modern notion of family is changing so nuclear families aren't always the best image of family in the postmodern world. The "nuclear family" terminology puts so much stress on immediate parental skills and child competence that families are actually threatened by this nuclear focus.[91]

The discussion is even further moved if the postmodern worldview is considered. In essence, Elkind states that the family has changed so much since the Bible days, we must redefine it so as to not over burden parents with parenting.

A third quote from the article sums up the conclusions and perhaps the underlying philosophical mindset behind much of traditional youth ministry.

> However, our understanding of Scripture leads us to recognize that the community of faith is the first family ministry that youth workers should be promoting.[92]

This emphasis away from promoting the nuclear family as preeminent to the family of faith is at the heart of the debate between the two Church models dealing with segregation or

---

[91] Ibid.
[92] Ibid.

integration.

The Family-Integrated Side

While the proponents of the age-segregated ministry in the above quotes highlight the family of faith and the necessity of separation between parents and children, the family-integrated model takes the exact opposite approach.

The argument is not about encouraging and participation within the family of faith, but rather, **who** has the primary responsibility for the spiritual development of the children.

George Barna sums up the philosophy in this excerpt;

> Parents who raised spiritual champions certainly placed a high premium on the spiritual development of their children. But the fascinating distinctive is that they saw themselves as the primary spiritual developers of their young ones.[93]

Under the family-integrated mindset, parents, and not the Church, are *primarily* responsible for the impartation of faith into the next generation. Barna also adds that the primary role of the organized church was to reinforce the parents' roles, not supplant them.

Jarrod Michel performed a survey of sixteen churches that adhere to the family-integrated ministry model for part of the requirements for the completion of his Master's degree from Denver Seminary. Michel sent an extensive interview form to the churches that agreed to participate in the study. These churches range in size from several families meeting together in a rural setting up to churches with over 2,000 members. The survey dealt with issues such as pastor education levels, church

---

[93] George Barna, *Revolutionary Parenting: What the Research Shows Really Works* (Carol Stream: Tyndale House Publishers, 2007), 57.

formation, government, worship style, and approach to ministry.[94] By sampling some of the respondents' answers and insights, we can gain some understanding of the age-integration philosophical mindset. The sixteen churches varied widely in the many areas surveyed, *except* on the family-integrated mindset and ministry application covered in the next section. All of the churches hold to the philosophical approach of non-segregation of the family into its various subsets per the typical age-segregated approach. All of the churches offer a family-centric, family-integrated approach to corporate church life. Within the churches, there is a variety of ways to implement the underlying philosophy, but all of the churches will maintain an integrated emphasis throughout.

Pastor John Nelson moved from a traditional age-segregated church to the family-integrated model and made this observation:

> I was directing the children, youth and adult ministries of churches and I realized one day that by taking the families apart and strengthening the pieces, but never putting them back together to make a stronger whole, that I was working against God's plan for the family as the basic building block of society. I was helping to facilitate individualism, and I was robbing each generation from the benefit of continual interaction with others of other generations.[95]

---

[94] Michel, Jarrod. 2008 Household Approach to Ministry; Rebuilding the Foundations of Family, Faith and Ministry. (Master's thesis, Denver Seminary)
[95] Ibid.,100.

Both Barna and Nelson capture the philosophical mindset of this Church model. The emphasis is placed on the parents to impart the Gospel to the children and on the Church to assist the parents, not visa-a-versa. There is a partnership needed, not a competition. This model insists that the church reinforces the parent's efforts and believes that if that happens both the family and the church will be stronger.

Jarrod's conclusion contains this thought:

> Therefore, rather than take over for the home, or make the home dependent upon the church for its spiritual wellbeing, the church ought to work alongside of the home - edify, encourage and support-with the intention of empowering the home to become a witness for Christ to others in the community, and an agent of the Church to help carry out the Great Commission. [96]

Needed Reflection

The implications of the Jarrod's research, as well as what is presented in this book, point to needed revaluation of the age-segregated approach in reaching the next generation for Christ. Change often happens slowly, but change is desperately needed. If the trends mentioned in the first chapter continue unabated, the Church will struggle to stay afloat and may even collapse. Perhaps an overstatement, then again, perhaps it is not. The Nehemiah Institute conducted a twenty-year survey based on a study of 60,000 students and reported these discouraging results:

> That secularization has successfully captured the hearts and minds of our youth rather than has the efforts of the Christian home, the church or even the traditional

---

[96] Ibid., 126

Christian school...it seems clear that the Christian Church could be in for a major collapse in the first half of the 21st century.[97]

The age-segregated church model invests huge sums of time and money attempting to capture the next generation, yet the results, according to the surveys quoted in this book, have been shown to be dismal. The implications of this research point to the need for serious evaluation of what is being accomplished using the currently accepted model. The famous saying applies here, "If you keep doing the same thing in the same way, you will keep getting the same results."

Those in the family-integrated movement see hope however, and the results (revealed shortly) have been encouraging so far. In the next section, we will look at some practical applications of how the family-integrated model actually functions in the local environment.

How Family-Integration Works in Practice

Since the word "family" or more accurately "family ministry" is used so often in reference to Churches, it would be good to examine in actual practice the differences between the two competing models. The age-segregated model has been referred to throughout the book, so we will develop the age-integrated model in this section for comparison purposes.

One unique distinctive of the family-integrated churches, is that the family is not segregated into its various components as soon as the family enters the building. The entire family is encouraged to experience the church service and most activities together. Children sit with the parents during the entire worship service, therefore nurseries, children's ministries, and youth specific services are not part of the church life. In fact, family-

---

[97] Ibid., 10

integrated churches are not departmentalized or centralized in the pastor(s) at all. Parents are encouraged to be the peer group of their children, and fathers are challenged to take the responsibility to lead and train their family. Specific teaching and training is directed to fathers and mothers to help them fulfill their Biblical roles, and the church resists interfering, or subverting those roles. The parents are expected to fulfill the role of the youth, children's, and singles' pastor and not delegate this task back to the Church. Dr. Doug Phillips sums it up well:

> I have the privilege of worshiping in a small, family-integrated church. When asked about our various church programs, I explain that we are blessed with more than thirty different organizations to which our members belong — they are called families. I further explain that we have more than sixty youth directors — they are called parents. In fact, we have such a full schedule of events that there is a mandatory activity every day of the week — it is called family worship.[98]

The Role of the Pastor

A philosophical shift as to the role of the pastor(s) occurs between the departmental, age-segregated, departmental model and the family-integrated one. Often in a departmental model, the congregation is encouraged to participate in the life of the church via activities and events, typically centered in the pastor or staff. For example, "the youth group will be taking a trip to Mexico," might be advertised in a church bulletin. On this trip,

---

[98] Doug Phillips, Esq., "Our Church Youth Group" 2002, Vision Forum Ministries, http://www.visionforumministries.org/issues/uniting_church_and_family/our_church_youth_group.aspx (accessed April 3, 2009)

the sponsoring church would provide leadership and staff, etc. Alternatively, there may be any number of causes, events, or programs that the church would want to emphasize, and they will usually provide staff to bring supervision and coordination for the event. Typical promotions will begin with, "Come join us as we..."

In a family-integrated model, families *still* go on a mission trip to Mexico and the pastor may or may not participate. The church might not even be involved. If asked, the church could assist with prayer or help make connections or assist with cash, but the initiative is parent driven, not staff driven. The focus is on what the family wants to do to provide an outreach for their children, not what the church wants to do to mobilize people. The same would be true for nursing home ministry, prolife work, evangelism, and children and youth ministry. The family is centric, not the church building or pastor. While this may seem unorthodox, the apostle Paul stated one of the jobs of the pastor was to "equip the saints to do the work of the ministry" in Ephesians 4:11-12. In the traditional age-segregated, departmental church, "equip" often means, we do, and you join us. In the family-integrated church "equip" means, you do, and we (church leadership) train and support.

Under this ministry model, the pastor's role changes from activity director and program initiator, to one that teaches the people how to do whatever ministry they are being led by God to perform. The pastor's job is to train the people through the teaching of the Scripture. The pastor explains to the people how to live a Christian life every day in the home, at school, and at the workplace. The philosophical mindset could be summed up in this statement: "ministry is birthed out of a functioning home." A home that is functioning according to Biblical principles will produce evangelism, outreach to the neighborhood, hospitality, missions, and a host of other service projects. From the home, families can conduct evangelism in their neighborhood, sing and teach at nursing homes, work in prolife counseling or political activities, take positions in the schools to support teachers, administration, and students, go to foreign countries to serve, work in food pantries, conduct small groups in their home, etc. All of these require little (budget or time wise) from the church or pastor, and is family driven in obedience to God's leading. The pastor trains, encourages, and releases. When the parents believe that their family is ready to serve, they serve as God directs. This does not mean that the pastor or church never does anything, but the *primary* responsibility for ministry comes from the home, not the organized church, or its leadership. When the church leadership believes that their church should do something, the opportunities are presented with the emphasis being placed on whether this is a fit for each individual family. No pressure is brought for every member to participate, but outreaches and events are available for those that care to participate. This reinforces the role of the parents as the leaders and initiators of their families' ministry endeavors.

The Typical Age-Integrated Church Service

A typical church service of a family-integrated church would not be very different from a family-segregated one. The primary difference would be *who* is in the service.
The children remain with their parents and are not isolated into groupings with their peers. Scott Brown, the director of the National Center for Family-Integrated Churches, comments as follows on Ephesians 6:

> In the first two verses, Paul is clearly speaking to children. These are the children who are in the meeting of the Ephesian church and are hearing the letter read. Paul uses a Greek grammatical form called the vocative case, called the "vocative of direct address." He is directly addressing the

children in the meeting of the church. This makes it an obvious fact that children were present in the meetings of the early churches.[99]

Some might argue that the children are not receiving any benefit from the teaching because they do not understand all of the words being spoken. The family-integrated proponents would disagree. The children are observing their parents and older siblings if they have them, and this observation can speak volumes. The child can learn the importance of worship as they observe their parents worship. The child can learn to respect the Word of God as they observe their parents' attentiveness to the teaching. The child can learn the importance of sitting quietly so others can listen. The child can learn the value of being together even if it is not entertaining or pleasurable. The child can learn that there are more important issues than simply their personal entertainment. Brown adds:

> Children progressively understand what a parent and the wider church members love and appreciate. Year after year, their understanding builds. Year after year, the well is filling up. The cumulative effect of deep and significant thinking and activities is what we are looking for.[100]

In reality, children do listen to what is being sung and taught. If they can understand words, they often will ask their parents about them as they think about them later. Many conversation opportunities take place as young children ask questions about

---

[99] Scott Brown, "Children in the Meeting of the Ephesian Church" 2004, Vision Forum Ministries, http://www.visionforumministries.org/issues/uniting_church_and_family/children_in_the_meeting_of_the.aspx (accessed April 3, 2009)
[100] Ibid.

something they either sang or heard during the service. This allows the father or mother to enter into a teaching mode with the children. These conversations allow adult level discussions to take place, which will help the child mature and develop mentally. These questions asked will also force the parents to be better prepared to answer them, thus helping to cement the pastor's message further into the mind of the parents. When children are isolated from the adults and taught by puppets or others at a very young level, it hinders the parents from having the opportunity to be the child's teacher and mentor. Many parents in the family-integrated churches will encourage their children to listen for specific words during the sermon and to write them down. Words like, "faith" or "joy" can easily be written and then discussed later with the children to assure they understand what was taught.

A final comment from Brown's article sums up the heart cry of many within the family-integrated model and notice that the family of faith is still important:

> We enjoy eating out together as a family. We enjoy going to the beach together as a family. Then, why do we not enjoy worship and instruction and fellowship as a family with our spiritual family of brothers and sisters?[101]

In the family-integrated model, relationships take precedence over programs and activities. Beyond the goal of strengthening the family relationships between parents and children, the marital relationship is valued and emphasized as central. When a marriage is falling apart through divorce, or simply reduced to a truce, rather than oneness that the Scripture calls for in Ephesians 5, the Gospel is hindered from going forth. A functioning home where both father and mother love each other is critical for evangelism, outreach, and a multigenerational

---

[101] Ibid.

impact. When the home falls apart, it has devastating results not only in the home, but also in the Kingdom of God. Thus, significant teaching and efforts will be invested in the family-integrated model to assist marriages through teaching, counseling, modeling and mentoring.

In addition, older children are encouraged to invest in the lives of younger children, thus promoting an inter-generational impact. The importance of an eighteen year old talking to and befriending an eleven year old can only be appreciated by remembering how we would have loved for it to happen to us when we were eleven. Integrating the ages from birth to grandparents can positively affect both the young and old. The potential for wisdom transference from older to younger is immense when everyone is comfortable with interacting. When each age is isolated to their own assemblage, it becomes increasingly difficult to find common ground or interest with those outside of your grouping. In the departmental, age-segregated model, it is unusual to observe the intergenerational interaction that is common in the family-integrated model.

As mentioned previously, there are hundreds of family-integrated churches being planted in every state and around the globe.[102] Similar to any other grouping of churches, there will of course be various means and methods to walking out this vision of integration. However, all of them will incorporate what was just written in some fashion or another. In addition, many churches are moving to this new model and are therefore in a hybrid status incorporating some of the underlying tenets as they transition out of an age-segregated model.

Noisy Children in Church

---

[102] As of April 1, 2009 there are currently 682 churches listed on The National Center for Family Integrated Churches website. http://ncfic.org/ (accessed April 1, 2009) This is not the only website for these type churches.

In addition to the typical objection of children not being able to understand the sermon, other issues often arise when considering the practical aspects of family-integrated ministry. The noise issue of children being in church is an example. Many pastors and adults simply do not want to deal with noisy children since they can be a distraction. In the family-integrated model, parents are encouraged to train their children to sit quietly during the service. This training typically takes place at home during the week. Children often sit for hours watching TV or coloring so it is not the lack of ability to sit quietly, but the lack of training on the parents' part to expect it from the children. Many family-integrated churches will offer a cry room or a place for parents to take their babies or toddlers to help them learn to become quiet. After the baby or child quiets down, the parents are encouraged to reenter the service and continue the training process. Most children can learn to sit still if the parents will train them. Of course, there are special needs children or undisciplined children that will need additional help and support. In the family-integrated church, often this is an opportunity for older children to assist another family by helping with the child, thus reinforcing the intergenerational goal.

Another argument presented is that the adults need to have time away from their children so they can learn the Bible undistracted. What is overlooked however, is that most parents have already spent huge blocks of time away from their children during the week. Fathers and mothers often work outside of the home, and the children go to school, so there has been significant time spent away from each other. The age-integrated model seeks to encourage more time being spent together not less. In addition, the families are encouraged to have family time during the week to discuss the Scripture, worship, and pray, thus promoting a godly center to the home. If these activities are taking place during the week, then it is perfectly natural for families to stay together during the larger congregational gathering.

The American family, by the nature of our hectic lifestyles, already experiences a significant amount of time away from each other. For example, many families participate in sports and other events, which sometimes require a major commitment of time and family segregation. The family-integrated mindset attempts to counter this trend beginning with the worship service. Alan Melton, the director of Family Together Ministries, states the problem of family dissection this way:

> There is a saying; "show me your checkbook, and I'll show you your priorities." Jesus said in Matthew 6:21, "For where your treasure is, there your heart will be also." What Jesus is saying is in essence "show me where you and your children spend your time, and I'll show you your priorities." THE PLACES WHERE YOUR CHILDREN SPEND THEIR TIME WILL BE WHAT WILL SHAPE THEIR LIVES. To sum it up, then most of our children's lives are being shaped by influences in the following order; school, Hollywood, peers, sports, church and in last place, parents.[103]

Outreach is Still the Goal

In summation of the practical outworking of the family-integrated model, the family is centric not the pastor or the church. The age isolation and segregation process is avoided in order to improve cross-generational influence and acceptance. Outreach, hospitality, missions and service projects, are parent

---

[103] Alan Melton, "Quality Time" 2007, The Association for the Restoration of Church and Home, ttp://www.restorechurchandhome.org/index.php?option=com_content&task=view&id=28&Itemid=32 (accessed April 3, 2009)

driven and not church leadership sponsored. However, the organized church can and should help facilitate, support, and train parents to succeed in their endeavors. The church leadership supports the parents and what they are attempting to accomplish in their family and does not compete with them. However, if there are sin issues or neglect involved, then of course the organized church has a Biblical responsibility to get involved with the situation and attempt to bring a godly solution.

The primary method of function within the family-integrated model is relational and not event or program driven. However, many events will take place as the families function in their own ministry. For example, within Hope Family Fellowship (a family-integrated church), there has been conducted a wide variety of ministry including: nursing home ministry, food pantry service, prolife support center workers, prison ministry, project Angel Tree (gifts to inmates families), Shoe Box Outreach (gifts to poor children around the world), backyard evangelism outreaches in neighborhoods, drama ministry, personal evangelism and discipleship, missions trips both in the US and abroad, service projects for single mothers and disabled fathers, worldview training, and many others, all birthed from the parental vision, not the church or its leadership.

While family-integrated ministry would seem to limit outreach and mission, the exact opposite is occurring. The natural outworking of a functioning home is outreach. A home in chaos has little to offer a hurting world. Where marriages are struggling to survive, and where children do not like their parents or each other, little of value can be exported. Where marriages are healthy and growing in oneness and where the parent child relationship is one of partnership, not adversarial, the normal result will be outreach and a desire to serve others. Thus, the family-integrated model's primary emphasis is placed on strengthening and encouraging the family as a whole, and not focusing on its individual components.

Some Encouraging Data

The problem of young people casting off their parent's faith as they leave the home after High School remains a grave matter of concern. As referenced earlier however, new data is coming out that should offer encouragement.

Brian D. Ray, Ph.D. recently published a study that analyzed over 7,000 adults that were home educated. Compared to the current failure ratio ranging between 70% - 90% that the Evangelical Church is experiencing in imparting their faith into the next generation (as shown in chapter one), the findings of this study are startling. Ray interviewed the adults and asked them a series of questions to which they could agree or disagree on a sliding scale. One question in particular highlights the findings, "94% strongly agreed, or agreed to the statement, "My religious beliefs are basically the same as those of my parents."[104] While the Evangelical Church is struggling to impart their faith into the next generation in huge numbers, this segment of the Church population is succeeding quite well.

Ray's conclusion presented in his study is also interesting:

> The findings of this study indicate that adults who were home educated are clearly engaged in their local communities and civic activity and will likely do so with a personal philosophy that is very similar to that of their parents and an attitude toward life that are different from the philosophy and attitude they might have learned in a state-run or private institutional school.[105]

---

[104]. Brian D. Ray PhD Ray, "Home Educated and Now Adults: Their Community and Civic Involvement" 2008, National Home Education Research Institute, http://www.nheri.org/Home-Educated-and-Now-Adults.html (accessed October 2, 2008).
[105]. Ibid.

Of course, research and interviews cannot conclusively prove that the parental interaction is *the* key to the retention of faith generationally, but it certainly does cause one to pause and think about the results.

These home-educated adults maintained not only the parent's faith, but also their sociological and political outlook.

Ray in another research project consisting of over 5,000 home-educated students, made this claim:

> More importantly, however, the lives of the home educated in decades to come and the heritage that they bequeath to their children may inscribe a sweeping, indelible, and immeasurable mark on the history of 21st-century America.[106]

This may be an overly optimistic claim; however, if the home education movement continues to maintain a 90% success rate in the impartation of the parent's faith and views into the next generation, perhaps it is not.

As previously mentioned, most families in the family-integrated church movement, also home educated their children. Having pastored a family-integrated church for almost twenty years, I am quite confident that the results will eventually be confirmed by future research. My church has over 350 in attendance and this includes a significant population of young people ranging from newborn to mid-twenties, which have not rejected their parents' faith. This, of course, is not proof, but it is an encouraging sign, nonetheless.

---

[106]. Dr. Brian Ray, "Strengths of Their Own," 2008, National Home Education Research Institute, http://www.nheri.org/strength-of-their-own.html (accessed October 2, 2008).

My Conclusions:

It is clear from the Scripture that God expects parents to be the primary source of training and education of their children in all matters, both spiritual and secular. There are numerous examples of parental oriented commands, but little recorded of the religious community's role in the process. In both the Old and New Testaments, the parents are primary. The Law and both Testaments instructed parents, and reinforced their position of responsibility for the faith impartation into their children. The Scripture lacks examples, or commands, regarding age-segregation, or any other isolation during the religious services, feasts, festivals, or congregational gatherings. Children seemed to be a part of everything, and parents were responsible for them, not the religious system. In fact, in the Old Testament, we observed that parents were often held responsible for the behavior of their adult children.

In the New Testament, we discovered that disobedience to parents was grouped with many other despicable sins, thus highlighting how God "thinks" about the parent-child relationship. Paul even instructed his young associates to disqualify a man from leadership if his family was not in proper order, and this seems to indicate adult level children.

The Scriptures also point out that the Church should be involved in assisting the parents with appropriate training to fulfill their roles, and also to provide a good role model for the family to imitate through its leadership. In light of this understanding, the partnership between the church and the home should be strengthened in order to return to a more historically Biblically understood methodology.

It seems clear that parents are commanded by God according to the Scripture to do everything possible to impart their faith into the next generation, and God will hold them responsible for their efforts. The Church is commanded by God through the Scripture, to do everything possible to reinforce the parental duty. When both parents and the Church work cooperatively, success can and will occur.

Thank you for reading my thoughts on this important topic. If I can be of service to you please contact me. May the Lord bless you and those you touch for Him.

Dr. Jeff Klick

APPENDEX - ARTICLES

The first article is a written transcript of an interview I did with Eric Burd, President of Household of Faith Churches for a national pastor's conference call. Many of the points in this discussion tie into the reasons for the family-integrated church model being my preferred one, and how I arrived at this conclusion.

Jeff, don't you think God intends a "familiness" to be present in the church?

Is God the CEO of the universe, or our Heavenly Father? Is Jesus the vice president in charge of human redemption, or our Savior and brother? Is the Holy Spirit the grand change agent for the human affairs department, or is He the One that integrates us into the family of God?

When we are born again, we become part of the family of God. We are not absorbed into a new corporation, but we enter into a family. We do not join a new movement but we enter into a family relationship. God is the One that came up with the design, not man. God is the One that said we are part of a body. We are the Bride of Christ. We are His children. God started the human story with a married couple, Jesus performed His first miracle at a wedding, and we are heading to the ultimate wedding as history ends. His idea. His plan.

Therefore, it would seem logical that God would have structured the organization of His church body along the same general pattern as He revealed Himself to us - like a family. The organized church today closely resembles a corporate structure more than a family one. Is this the plan revealed in Scripture?

Why do you think the church today looks more like a corporation than a family?

The church has not always functioned this way. We in the FIC movement, sometimes tend to think we created something new, but what we really have done is return to something old. The separating of the family into age groups is a relatively new concept compared to the scope of church history. In the 1950-60's, a school of thought arose along the Youth for Christ mindset that found great success. I am not knocking it, just reporting here.

Pre-1950's there really was not that much thought even given to teenagers as a stage of life. They were simply young adults and expected to act like adults. As groups started to form that focused on the teenagers, there began a gradual downward spiral into more juvenile and isolated thinking. The popularity of these groups caught the attention of the church. The church began to adopt some of these methods and the modern youth emphasis was in full swing.

If you perform a simple Google search today on youth or children's ministries, you will find thousands of them. Full curriculums, how-to seminars, leadership training, and a host of supporting ministries have sprung up. A mindset has been adopted that in order to be successful as a church, the youth must be served.

Studies are quoted that state that if you fail to reach the young people before the age of eighteen, they will not be reached. So children's ministries, age-segregated Sunday schools, junior youth, senior youth, college and career, singles, and just about any other age division you can think of, are common. If a church hopes to be relevant and attractive to the modern family, ministry must be supplied for the children.

Thus, enter the corporate mindset?

As the church attempted to reach the young people, more structure was required. A solo teaching pastor was not going to be gifted or able to reach the children, youth, singles, and other groups effectively. The church had to grow and adapt. Staff had to increase. Support staff had to be added to help the staff reach the various groups. Larger buildings were needed to support the growth of families that were willing to allow the church staff to train their children.

As the church grew and became popular, more structure was needed. The days of one pastor studying, praying, and visiting his members were quickly becoming a distant memory. Ministry was being redefined and quantified. Numerical growth, facilities, staff size, and outreach all became the goal. Again, I am not calling into question the motives of anyone, just reporting historical facts.

Part of what happened was some churches became huge. New terms were coined, like mega-church and hyper-growth. These became the visible ministries that purchased TV and radio time. Success breeds imitation. This ministry model became THE ministry model. Young pastors wanted to become the next mega-ministry to leave their mark on the world.

Seminaries began to teach young students this model is the one that will lead to success. A large staff, huge budget, growing congregation, and ever-present facility expansion became the norm. More than the norm, it became the plumb line for success. Attend any pastor's meeting and walk up to a pastor and after the name is given, the next question will almost always be - "How big is your church?"

The bigness of a church demands structure and organization. Department heads, countless volunteers, payroll, financing, fund raising, maintenance, and clerical staff became a need. The church had arrived at the pinnacle of success. Millions of dollars and hundreds of employees demands organization. Leadership seminars and books proliferated. How-to's from those who had achieved the results, became must reading. Speakers, seminars, conferences, training, all in the quest for success became standard training for church leaders.

While none of these things is necessarily wrong, it makes one wonder about what happened to the pastor's study, prayer time, and personal relationships. A pastor will receive a great deal of training in leadership but how much in effective prayer? The ins and outs of advance fund raising and staff management are required but how much in developing personal relationships? It is easy today for a corporate executive to move into the pulpit and the lead pastor's role because the functions are not that much different, just the end product and dollar amounts.

Here is something that I call a dirty little secret - this model produces activity because of job security and not necessarily results achieved. Every staff person must produce and earn their share of the budget or their job will be in jeopardy. Thus, you have an explosion of meetings, outreaches, and events in order to justify the salary paid. We must stay busy or we will be out on the street. This breeds infighting, competition, and many times strife over money, people, and face time before the congregation. The vision of the church is often fractured around strong personalities and individual visions.

You seem to know something about all of this - can you explain your background a bit?

In the late 1970's, I began working for H & R Block. I managed 32 tax offices for them and wanted to become the youngest divisional director in the company's history. As I was pursuing this goal, God called me to walk away from it. I did not know what He had in mind, but I was not too happy. We ended up going to a large church in KC where I noticed an advertisement for help with the bookkeeping. I offered to assist and shortly thereafter, the church offered me the position of church administrator.

During the next eleven years, I worked like crazy. We grew from 1100 to 3500 attendees. I helped build the infrastructure of this church. Hired the department heads, associate pastors, was in charge of basically everything from the facilities to being the elder in charge of the Christian school. I taught, led the staff, had dozens of meetings, and basically ran on adrenalin overload for over a decade. I was able to build the ultimate church structure and we were hugely successful. We had a network of over 40 churches and we were the hot spot in KC.

In 1993, the senior pastor ran off with his book editor and chaos reigned. During my final few months there, many of my views of what a pastor should do were challenged. Actually, this evaluation time had begun a few years earlier, but now these thoughts were being forced into the forefront.

A couple of years before this, I had begun to question the wisdom of what we built. One event stood out in my mind as I revisit all of this. I took a week once to interview the 120 junior and senior students at our Christian school. Out of these young people, I found just a few that really loved the Lord. This struck me as sad since we had these young people under our care since birth. Where had we failed to reach them? We were spending over 1/3 of a million dollars a year on the school and the young people were hard as a rock toward the Lord. Why?

I have since learned that this is not a unique finding. Studies show that 70-90% of young people walk away from their faith by the first year in college. How could this be? In my world, we had the best nursery, children's ministry, junior and senior youth leaders, and college leaders that money could hire. How could we be losing these young people in such huge numbers?

As I contemplated the changes coming to my personal world, I began to entertain some new thoughts. What did the Bible actually say the job of a pastor was anyway? I knew what I had been doing, but what did the Scripture specifically say? If I ever started a church, what would it look like in function and vision? If the fruit of what we were doing was so poor, what could we do differently? These are dangerous thoughts indeed.

In December 1993, Hope Family Fellowship was birthed. Our goal was to not do much of what the corporate church had decided was required to be successful. The goal switched from being financially and corporately successful to helping families take the responsibility for their own spiritual development and discipleship. I would challenge fathers to lead their families. In fact, I would resist having them delegate that responsibility to me as the pastor and to the church organizationally.

We did not find out that we were called a family-integrated church until the early 2000's. Up until then, we thought we were alone and just plain weird.

How did you come to these conclusions about family integration?

The question I had to answer was if a church were not going to be corporate in structure, how would it operate? As I studied this, it became clear that much of what I had been doing was not mandated in the Scripture. In fact, there is a procedure used to help us think differently called "The Desert Island View." This method would be good to run some of our ideas through on a regular basis. Here is a quick summary:

If the Bible washed up on a deserted island and was found by someone who had never seen one before what would they do based on what they read? If the reader had no preconceived ideas of how "church" should be performed, what would it look like? While we cannot know for sure, no serious thinker would come up with an age-segregated, corporate model from the pages of Scripture. Nowhere within the pages of Scripture is a reader going to find what we do today as church. In neither Testament will the family being separated into parts come into focus. The family is always primary and almost always intact. There are no youth groups, children's, or single groups mentioned, but the family is centric and primary on nearly every page.

In the Old Testament, using either the tabernacle or the temple model, the family is usually either all together or the father represents the whole unit. It was unheard of to isolate the various segments of the family. The same pattern is true in the New Testament. There is no mandate for the organized church to isolate. The picture presented in both Testaments is a family unit serving God together. The father is leading and the family is in step with him. While there is an organizational structure in the Old Testament, even this is always tied to the father. God's people in both Testaments were strictly warned to not imitate the unbelievers around them. The modern church has largely ignored the warning.

By adopting a corporate mindset in the church, has the role of the father been diminished?

The simple answer is yes. The currently popular church model, while I believe it is unintentional, has almost entirely removed the father from leading his home. Parents can delegate away their responsibility to the "professionals" at the local church and honestly believe they are doing the best thing for the family. These staff pastors/leaders are highly trained and they know how to reach the children, or so the thinking goes. Never mind that every study proves the failure of this method - the myth continues. The typical youth leader is just slightly more mature than those being led.

That is probably harsher than it needs to be stated, but still, the proof is in the fruit produced. Marriages are falling apart and young adults are leaving the church in record numbers. If something does not change quickly, the church is in deep trouble. I am not full of fear because I know Jesus said He would build the church and it will not fail. However, that growing church is largely moving away from the country that I love.

To be honest, the corporate mindset is not entirely the fault of the church. The delegation of the training responsibility to the church provides a measure of insulation later on for the parents, and I believe that is why so many choose this model. "We did the best we could. We sent them to the finest schools and church programs, so it is not our fault that they walked away. What else could we do?" says the broken parent when their child rejects Christ.

How entrenched is this view and church model?

Those of us who have attempted to challenge the status quo have been criticized, marginalized, and demonized. We have been called extremist. We are told we worship the family. We are Amish-like and ruining our children through withholding what is so obviously good for them. This all sounds like the abuse we early homeschoolers endured as well.

Some of us have pursued advanced degrees and ventured into the academic foray. My Ph.D. dissertation was entitled, *The Biblical Analysis of the Roles of the Family and Church Regarding Faith Impartation*. One has to love the titles of such things. My basic argument went along the lines of the current church model is clearly failing, so why don't we go back and look at Scripture to see what it really says?

My lead professor had earned his degrees in Christian education and I was attacking this as unbiblical. Our relationship was tense, to put it mildly. The understanding that the Scripture presents a clear family-oriented society seemed to be a strange concept. Historical writings, Scripture quotations, examples, and objective research really did not go over too well. After about a year-and-a-half battle, my final draft was approved, but I think they just wanted to get rid of me.

The model is entrenched because it seems to work. It works, that is, if money, numbers, large staff, and buildings is the goal. If effective generational transference of the faith is a goal, it fails miserably.

So if this current model is not really biblical, what should a local church do?

I believe we must abandon the corporate mindset. The pursuit of numbers, money, and activity must be changed into the desire to see a healthy functioning home. That is, if the family is the primary tool used by God to propagate the faith, and it is. If the family is the glue that holds together the society around us, and it is. If the family structure is the plan and preferred model from God in the beginning, and it was, we must rethink what we are doing.

Yes, we must reach the young people with the Gospel before they reach adulthood, but **who** should reach them is the correct question. Whom did God place in their life with the best opportunity, the most access time, and natural relationship? Even the busiest church in the country only has the children for a few hours a week. The parents have access that every pastor could only dream about. A captive audience that had to listen.

Most pastors would love to have someone attend a discipleship class that lasts six weeks.

How long does a father have access to his children? Every meal is an opportunity. Each day is a possibility to impart to the next generation. We must not waste it.

"But what about service projects and ministry?" the department head asks. Great question. What would happen if each pastor began to challenge every family under their care to reach out to those around them in love? Every person in the pew knows people that the pastor or staff member will never be able to reach, but they could. What would happen if families actually began to do the work of the ministry instead of the paid staff only?

A mindset must change if this is going to happen. I hear rumblings of it and I am very grateful. Authors like David Platt and others are getting press for their "radical" ideas. These ideas are pretty commonplace in the FIC world, but let us rejoice if they receive a larger hearing and acceptance.

Part of my soul searching during my transition time was based around Ephesians 4:11-12. This is one of the few places that the job of the pastor is actually expounded. Verse 12 says we are to "equip the saints to do the work of the ministry," and here is where the mindset needs to change.

In the corporate structure, this equipping takes place from the staff's point of view and at their initiation. In the large church where I served, we would schedule an event or outreach and invite the masses to come along with us. We would promote, attempt to train somehow and conduct the event. The results were almost secondary to the activity itself. "We had five hundred people go out witnessing," boasts the evangelism pastor. "We handed out thousands of tracts." Of course that is great! However, if those same five hundred people had been inviting their neighbors over for a cookout and evening of fellowship and getting to know one another, would the results be higher or last longer? Which event would lead to more relationships and the possibility of discipleship?

What would have happened to the children's view of their father as he was observed sharing his faith with the neighbor? What about the mother, or the children, as they helped get everything ready to share their faith? The evangelism pastor may not have had as big or seemingly successful event, but I wonder in the great scope of things, which way would produce the best, longest-lasting fruit. I really don't have to wonder, for the statistics are clear.

God created the family as the primary model for the Church to imitate.

Why focus so much on the family? I did an informal survey, knowing full well the results before I even asked. I polled pastors, asking, "How much of your counseling time is spent in dealing with dysfunctional family issues such as marriage counseling, parent/child issues, etc." As expected, the vast majority of the time spent dealt with the breakdown of the family. The next question is often not asked, but must be - what are we doing about it? I asked this question one time to the fifteen pastors under my leadership and all I received was blank stares.

My premise is that a great deal of ministry flows from a functioning home and very little from a dysfunctional one. If effective ministry is the goal, where should our emphasis be focused as leaders? If we are to be effective in equipping the saints, we must cast off the corporate model and get back to the basics of helping the family flourish. Dividing the family into its parts simply is not the best method to accomplish the God-given task to pastors/elders of equipping those under their care.

If the church is a family, and she is, then following the family model would make the most sense. Far more sense than following corporate America. Families have a more fluid structure, and they are primarily relationship-based. Churches should be relationship-based as well. The kingdom of God is relational at the root level.

We have a relationship with our Father and we are part of a living group called the body of Christ.

Being born again is a family term. We were born the first time into a family, and when we are saved, we are born again into a new family. We have a new Father and millions of new brothers and sisters. We do not join the great corporation of Christ but we become part of His bride. In any family, there is structure. Biblically speaking, the father is the under-shepherd to the family, leading under the great Shepherd. In the church, God has called pastors/elders to provide leadership and oversight.

The goal of a wise father is to train his children and to prepare them to leave the comfort of the home to make a difference for Christ. The same should be true for the leadership of the local church. The pastor/elder should be equipping the saints to do the work of the ministry. Train and release. Prepare and send out. The most logical place for the pastor/elder to invest his time is with the head of the family.

I realize that there are many families that are already dysfunctional. The tragedy of divorce and absent fathers is wreaking havoc. But, the correction of abuse is not disuse but proper use. We cannot minister by exception but by vision and principle. We deal with exception but we should order the church based on clear biblical principles. The family model is clear.

We hurt with and assist those without the family intact, but we do not throw out the model because of them. In fact, the best help for dysfunction is to model proper function. Healthy families are the cure for sick ones. Integration is part of the solution and help needed to repair what is damaged.

Further isolation is not helpful. We must model what is correct to change what is damaged.

So, Jeff, for our HOFCC reform, Household-Like in Structure, we define that as: organizing the structure and activities of our HOFCC church along the simple lines of loving, well-ordered, age-integrated households. It sounds like that explanation would be a fit for your church at Hope Family Fellowship in Kansas City as well?

Exactly, Eric, this has always been our model as well. In fact I have gone through this interview with the very purpose of showing the contrast between contemporary models and what it seems that God had in mind for the church from the beginning.

Our churches ARE our extended family, and the ideal is when we experience the joy and fellowship of what God has designed for us. As churches we should more-or-less function as an extended family.

A)   The church is the "household" of God.
B)   God is our "Father."
C)   Christ is the "firstborn" and our "Elder Brother."
D)   Leaders are "elders" of the family.
E)   We are all "brothers & sisters."

Galatians 6:10 So then, <u>while we have opportunity,</u> let us <u>do good to all people</u>, and <u>especially to those</u> who are of <u>the household of the faith</u>.

This emphasis allows us to avoid institutionalism while maintaining an orderly structure that encourages our ministry to be more of a loving lifestyle.

We have returned to a more relationship base rather than an institutional base. We are really not program-oriented. Ministry takes place in the context of relationships, and I would argue in a more efficient manner with a longer impact than anything I ever accomplished through the corporate structure model. The primary difference is it is age-integrated and family-directed, and not commanded from the leadership. Pastors/elders should invest the bulk of their time in supporting the family to be healthy. The fathers should be the primary target for training and follow-up so they can take that training and lead those under their care. This does not mean that mothers and children are never addressed or given specific training, but the leadership should invest in the leader of the home first, and often, if long-term change is to be gained.

About a year after starting Hope Family Fellowship, I had a meeting with the elders of the large church I had left. As we chatted, I shared one important principle learned. "When I served at this church I used people as a means to an end. Now I know the people are the end." An awkward silence followed.

The local church should support the family unit, not divide it. You will be hard pressed to find any examples of age-segregation in the Scripture. You will however find examples of a unified family unit in just about every book. By staying together in worship and ministry, families actually model the philosophy of ministry God has established for both church and family.

If God set up the family the way He did, if God wrote the Scripture the way He did, if down through the centuries the family has always been primary, why are we abandoning it now? Is the age-segregated, department-dominated model really a biblical one? I do not believe so. The family model is, so why are we not following it? Why would we separate the children from the parents on Sunday? Why would we want to remove the primary responsibility of teaching away from the parents and onto a church staff? Why would we want to deprive the father the joy of leading his children to salvation?

Why would we want to create activities to keep the family busy instead of helping each family fulfill its unique calling from the Lord?

We would not, and that is why we are FIC.

Dr. Jeff Klick

http://www.hofcc.org/ -This is Eric's website for the Household of Faith Fellowship of Churches. Please check them out to see if there is one near you!

****

This second article is a written version of a presentation given to a group of pastors in the Kansas City area and attempts to broaden the discussion regarding the typical church staff.

Rethinking Church Staff Positions:

Eph 4:11-12 - And he gave the apostles, the prophets, the evangelists, the pastors and teachers, to equip the saints for the work of ministry, for building up the body of Christ (ESV).

The idea in this verse is that as under-shepherds, we are to be about the business of correcting what is wrong in doctrine, theology, thought patterns encompassing orthodoxy and orthopraxy, and to strengthen and encourage what is healing and redemptive.
Most of us would probably agree that the family unit is broken, or at least in need of strengthening/repair. Divorce statistics for the church at large are close to same as the people that are not born again. Young people are leaving the church in droves.

153

Churches are closing every day and few would argue that we do not have a major problem on our hands in the Church.

I have not performed the research, but based on the last 30 years of experience I would venture to say that the bulk of my counseling time has been devoted to the breakdown of the marriage (communication, $ and sexual issues) and parent/child relational issues.

I have performed detailed doctoral research on what the Bible contains regarding the roles of parents and the organized religious intuitions regarding faith impartation to the next generation. The results were staggering. There are few direct commands to the church either in the New, or in the sanctuary/temple patterns of the Old, regarding the organized religious community's role. There are hundreds directed towards the parent's role and responsibilities, in addition to a great deal of Scripture addressing the marriage relationship.

Perhaps God intended that the parents take the leadership role in such things and that the leaders of the organized community come alongside them to supplement. The traditional family unit is broken and in need of significant repair. What are we, who are charged with leading God's people, doing about it? If we are serious about reversing the destruction of the family unit, perhaps some new ministry departments or staff positions should be considered as well:

- Staff in charge of strengthening the father in his leadership role in the home
- Pastor in charge of training husbands to love their wives as Christ loved the Church
- Malachi 4:6 curse avoider trainer
- Encouraging the wives and mothers in their Biblical mandate counselor
- How not to destroy your home by your words consultant

- How to be more Christ-like with those that know you best, pastor
- Family devotions to implement the pastor's message during the week advisor
- Marriage Stability and Longevity Coordinator
- Divorce prevention pastor
- Reducer of Hypocrisy in the home consultant
- Preparation for being a godly spouse trainer
- Teenage rebellion avoidance ministry leader
- Sibling relationships enhancer
- Helping young people make wise, godly decisions under their parent's authority director
- Giving single adults a purpose in life by serving others leader
- Grandparents as support to parents and not undermine minister

Perhaps you could think of some others. Research indicates that we often spend a great deal of time and money on recovery programs but not all that much on prevention. While parking ambulances at the bottom of the cliff is helpful, stronger guardrails at the top would also seem in order.

The family is the central unit of society and is the plan that God established in His Word for continuity in the faith. Fathers and mothers explaining the truths of God's word to their children is the clear pattern repeated throughout the pages of our Holy Book. God chose a family model out of all the possible ones, being call Father instead of CEO of the universe, or Supreme Executive. He sent His Son, not the VP in charge of Humanity. We are adopted into the family of God; we do not become shareholders of the human corporation. We have many brothers and sisters instead of business partners and again, we are adopted, not merged, absorbed, or taken over. Adam and

Eve were the first family, Jesus was born into one, and all of time will end with a marriage feast between Christ and His bride. The traditional family is centric to Christianity, and its continuance.

If we are to turn the tables on the destruction of the family, we should begin to rethink what our goals are and how to go about implementing change. What specifically am I doing to stem the tide of destruction? Every destroyed family unleashes generational destruction; what will every restored one produce? A partial answer based on practical observation is, that a great deal of effective ministry will come from a functioning home, and very little from a messed up one. As marriages are healed, and relationships restored within the home, outreach to others is a very natural result. A parent reaching their children for Christ is a wonderful fulfillment of the last verse of our Old Testament. This also helps fulfill the great commission. Training our people to reach the potential disciples right under their roof will give good practice as they go out into the highways and byways. Leadership skills learned in the home do transfer to the organized church and world around us. Strong leaders at home can become strong leaders in the Church.

I could go on to qualifications for elders/deacons being tied to the family. How marriage is a picture of the mystery of Christ and the Church. How prayers are hindered by husband/wife relational problems. How power is released when two agree together. How Biblically we cannot delegate away our parenting responsibilities. The stewardship responsibilities tied to our families given by God, etc. but time restraints affect us all. My prayer is that as those charged with fixing things that are broken, we would begin with the ones closest to us, and that we would capture the harvest that is white within our own fields, before we go to far off ones.

This third article was a positive response to a negative presentation regarding the family-integrated movement. I present it here because it explains many of reasons of why are we are attempting to change the currently popular model, and some of the resistance we face.

United Families Dividing Churches

A Response to Dr. Brown's Article Regarding FICM

First, we would congratulate Dr. Brown on his well-written article and commend him on his reasonable presentation. There is much to be agreed upon as well as some areas to clarify.

The FICM movement is indeed making progress and is having an impact in many areas of the country. With the goal of restoration of the family at its core, it is hard not to have a measure of success given the dismal condition of the family unit in our time. Families are the heartbeat of the nation and church, and they are falling apart in record numbers. The fallout continues to be disastrous to both Christ's name, and on those torn apart from the pain and heartache. Any sincere effort to help stop the tide of destruction must be applauded.

My own (Jeff Klick) FIC church was planted in December 1993 as a direct result of seeing the "fruit" of eleven years of ministry in a more traditional, department-oriented church. After feeling powerless to make a difference in so many families' lives, we decided to take a new path to help restore the family unit. I am grateful for the experience received in age-segregated type ministry for it became the foundation for trying something different.

Not all FIC proponents are hostile to the currently acceptable methods of ministry that dominate the church structures. Nor do all of us regard the current model of age-segregation as evil. In fact, many FIC churches typically practice some sort of age-segregation through men's and women's meetings, and other age/gender appropriate type teaching settings, like Bright Lights, Boy Scouts, or sports teams.

The leaders you mentioned are the most well known, but they are by no means the only men attempting to minister to the family unit in this ministry model. As you correctly stated, "the FICM is not a denomination" and therefore the generalities you mentioned are simply that, general statements. These men have their views but they do not necessarily reflect the entire picture or views of many leaders across the nation.

While serving as an administrative pastor for a large church (3,500 members) I (Jeff) had the opportunity to interact with hundreds of young people and their parents. I served as a youth pastor for two years, an elder (pastor) in charge of our Christian school (600 students) and was instrumental in designing the departmental approach to the entire ministry. This period allowed me the opportunity to see the results of the church's impact through our ministry over a ten-year window. We had many of the children in our programs from the time they were born until the time they left the church. Our results would be in line with most of the studies you mentioned. We had invested millions of dollars and thousands of man-hours, yet the rate of faith rejection was on the high end. While we may argue over the reasons why, the truth of the rejection cannot be ignored. A large percentage of the young people walked away from Christ by the time they finished high school, even though they had been in our programs from birth. This reality prompted some soul searching and became the seedbed of a desire to attempt a different type of ministry.

Since there is much we agree on, it would be better to move on to Dr. Brown's evaluation and summary comments regarding this new ministry model. First, I would concur with Dr. Brown's five areas of agreement with the FICM churches. Most are Biblically oriented, Christ-centered, Church loving, holiness desiring, and are attempting to address the fundamental problem of family destruction. These are indeed some things to be grateful for in the new movement.

Dr. Brown is correct in his hesitancy about making dogmatic statements on Biblical silence. Neither age-segregation nor integration is specifically addressed in Scripture, although the fact that Paul addresses children in his letters to the Colossian and Ephesian churches gives rise to the idea that these same children would have been present in the public gathering for worship, when the Apostle's letter was to be read. The Bible supports the idea that the family is the fundamental building block of society, but that does not mean that every Church that practices age-segregation is in error. On this, we would agree. Biblical silence on specifics regarding age-segregation or integration also means that age-integration is not forbidden, nor should this model be regarded with disapproval because it is different.

As Dr. Brown states, "The mandate to "make disciples" is given to the church (Matt. 28:19, 20)," but if we are to be technical at this point, the command was actually given to Jesus' disciples and to those watching Him ascend into heaven. If by "Church" Dr. Brown means the organized church rather than the individuals that make up the church, then we will have to agree to disagree. The organized church did not develop until a bit later. At this point (when Jesus gave His final commission to His followers), the disciples were told to go, and make disciples. After they went proclaiming the Gospel, issues were encountered, for example, it took some time to figure out what to do with the Gentile problem (Acts 15), how to take care of the poor (Acts 6), who was to lead, how to deal with false prophets, etc.

These issues and others had to be dealt with long before the Church settled into some sort of unified form, so to state that the exclusive job of discipling is the territory of the organized church is not entirely accurate. The command to make disciples is everyone's job, and not simply the responsibility of the leadership of the organized church.

We would concur with Dr. Brown regarding the teaching ministry of the Church and its value to equipping the saints for ministry. One of the primary roles of the leadership of the Church should be the impartation of Biblical, life-changing truth. The best place to learn how to walk out that truth is in the home.

We see this call for fathers to disciple their own children as a fundamental truth throughout Scripture. Deuteronomy 6:4-9 is a command to the fathers in Israel to love the Lord with all their heart, and the measure of that love will be the training of their children to do the same. God says to Dads, *You shall teach them* (His commands) *diligently to your children, and shall talk of them when you sit in your house, when you walk by the way, when you lie down, and when you rise up.* (Deuteronomy 6:7)

Proverbs was written by a young father who saw it was his responsibility under God to train his son. *My son, hear the instruction of your father, and do not forsake the law of your mother.* (Proverbs 1:8) Solomon calls on his son again in chapter 2 to listen to his teaching: *My son, if you receive my words, and treasure my commands within you…* (Proverbs 2:1). Again in chapters, 3,4,5,6 and 7, Solomon begins his teaching with a word to his son! Solomon did not hand over his responsibility for spiritual training to the priests and the scribes; he did it himself. In the New Testament, the principle is repeated: *And you, fathers, do not provoke your children to wrath, but bring them up in the training and admonition of the Lord.* (Ephesians 6:4)

This does not mean the church has no role in the discipling the children. Indeed, we believe God has ordained a perfect marriage between family and church. The pastors and elders are to equip the saints for the work of the ministry (Ephesians 4), and the fathers, being equipped by the church leaders, are to teach their own sons and daughters to love God with all their heart, soul and strength. What is taught in the Church should be walked out in real life, and especially in the family unit. What would happen if the home actually did take the truth taught from the Church and implemented it daily in the home? What would happen to the family structure if the parents took notes on the teaching received and discussed these everyday with the family until the next meeting?

I (J. Mark Fox) can tell you what has happened in the twenty years Antioch Community Church has been family integrated. Children have grown up loving the Lord Jesus into their adulthood. We have lost none of the teenagers who grew up in this model and went away to college. We have also seen men rise to the challenge of leading their marriages and homes in the Word, teaching and training their primary disciples and giving them a vision for serving the Lord. In twenty years, there has been only one marriage that ended in divorce. This is anecdotal evidence, for sure, but it is also strong fruit, the kind of fruit that Jesus said His followers would bear, "fruit that remains." (John 15:16) I believe the key to this fruit is that these men have been in a church that did not make a way for them to abdicate their responsibilities, and instead encouraged them and equipped them to fulfill, with great joy, their leadership in the home. I am reminded of a statement E.M. Bounds made in his book, *Power Through Prayer*: "What the Church needs today is not more machinery or better, not new organizations or more and novel methods, but men whom the Holy Ghost can use -- men of prayer, men mighty in prayer. The Holy Ghost does not flow through methods, but through men. He does not come on machinery, but on men. He does not anoint plans, but men -- men of prayer."

Discipleship is the goal and the FIC community primarily believes that the parents are the best ones to train the children, to which Dr. Brown stated he agrees. Who better to lead the children to Christ than the ones charged by God to bring them up in the nurture and admonition of Lord? (Ephesians 6:4) The parents will have an opportunity to interact with the child for almost two decades. How many hours does the organized Church have per week with the children? The organized Church should be providing wonderful materials and instruction for the practical application of Christianity to be walked out every day in the home. It is a perfect partnership.

It would be impossible to prove where and why someone actually rejects Christ via studies and interviews. Blaming an organizational structure is an easy scapegoat, yet in light of the dismal results being experienced in faith retention, nothing should be overlooked, including structures. It is more likely that most young people reject Christ because they did not see the power or reality of their parent's personal walk. Many studies point to hypocrisy in the home as the primary cause of teen rejection of Christ. Regardless of structure, if parents claim to be believers in Jesus Christ, yet there is no noticeable difference in how they live their daily lives, the young people observing them will most likely reject the need for salvation. As one young agnostic told me (Jeff) so clearly, "My parent's faith made no difference in their life. Why should I even bother with it?" He had a point that we should not overlook.

Have there been judgmental, even inflammatory statements made by some proponents of the FICM? Sadly, yes. We believe their motives are good ones, in that their greatest concern is for the Gospel and for the next generation to run the race with endurance, but at times their zeal has provoked offense in the larger body of Christ. For these overstatements, we would ask those offended to please forgive and bear with the insensitive, overstated comments. There is a great deal to be gained by working together and little by separating and fighting.

On the other hand, many within the FIC model have felt pushed out of the Church by the current age-segregated leaders. Pressure is put on the family to divide as soon as the family hits the door, and some would rather leave than endure the looks and comments from well-meaning ushers, or pastors. Some families have been told, "You may not bring your children into the sanctuary with you. We have another place for them." Hurtful comments aimed at families who have a conviction about family integrated worship range from the number of children they have to other personal choices such as clothing styles, education choices, lack of familiarity with pop culture, and a host of other non-Biblical issues. Pressure is put on children and teens by Sunday School teachers, youth leaders, and others to break away from the parents even though the family has clearly decided to worship and serve together. Respect for personal preferences should go both ways. It is easy to blame one side with causing division, but the truth is there is a need for more communication, sensitivity, and understanding on both sides.

Our partnership is in the Gospel of Jesus Christ, whether we believe in the FICM or in age-segregation. We have more common ground than ground upon which we disagree. Our common goal is to see Jesus Christ glorified, the people of God edified, and the lost reached with the good news of the Gospel. We in the FICM do not elevate the family over the church, but believe that the church and family should work together for the glory of God. The fruit of family integrated churches that have been faithfully equipping families and singles over the past twenty years is hard to ignore. We even believe it should be respected and celebrated in the larger body of Christ.
In Christ,

C4FIC
Jeffrey A. Klick, Ph.D. Board Member

J. Mark Fox Board Member - http://www.antiochchurch.cc/ - This is Mark Fox's church website. Mark is an excellent brother that has a similar journey to mine.

ABOUT THE AUTHOR

Jeff and Leslie Klick live in Shawnee, Kansas and have three adult children and ten grandchildren. Jeff has been in full-time ministry for over thirty years.

www.jeffklick.com - Dr. Klick's blog and personal website
www.hopefamilyfellowship.org - Dr. Klick's church website

In addition to being a pastor, Dr. Klick serves the Body of Christ through radio and technology outlets including The Alive in Christ Radio Network. On Tuesday evenings, Dr. Klick serves as one of the pastors during a teaching time discussing discipleships. Wednesdays Dr. Klick can be heard on a radio show called Christian Business 360, which is geared to assisting Christian Business people, and on Fridays he can be seen on a live Google+ TV discussion involving leaders from around the country.

Dr. Klick also serves as an instructor for the Institute of Church Management and is on the board of The Council for Family-Integrated Churches. Recently, Dr. Klick has collaborated with Trinity Seminary to begin Trinity Discipleship Institute, which offers 24 on-line classes for those that desire a deeper education in the Word of God.

Dr. Klick's other books:
Courage to Flee; Living a Moral Life in an Immoral World
Generational Impact; A Vision for the Family
Saints Under Construction; We are all a Masterpiece in Process
The Discipling Church; Equipping, Empowering the Body of Christ

BIBLIOGRAPHY

Adeney, W. F. "Deuteronomy." In *The Pulpit Commentary*. Electronic Edition STEP Files. Reprint, AGES Library, Association of Christian Schools International. "2007 ACSI Annual Report," 2007. http://www.acsi.org/webfiles/webitems/attachments/002991_2 007 Annual Report.pdf.

Augustine - Chapter 22.—Of the Miseries and Ills to Which the Human Race is Justly Exposed Through the First Sin, and from Which None Can Be Delivered Save by Christ's Grace. http://www.ccel.org/ccel/schaff/npnf102.iv.XXII.22.html?high light=children,school#highlight

Barna, George. "Most Twentysomethings Put Christianity on the Shelf Following Spiritually Active Teen Years," September 11, 2006. http://www.barna.org.

Barna, George. The Power of Vision: How You Can Capture and Apply God's Vision for Your Ministry. Ventura, California: Regal Books, 1992.

Barna, George. *Revolution*. Carol Stream, Illinois: Tyndale House Publishers, 2005.

Barna, George *Revolutionary Parenting: What the Research Shows Really Works* Carol Stream: Tyndale House Publishers, 2007.

Baxter, Richard. "Biblical Parenthood." *Free Grace Broadcaster* 208 (Summer 2008).

Becker, Penny Edgell. *Congregations in Conflict, Cultural Models of Local Religious Life*. New York, New York: Cambridge University Press, 1999.

Bennett, William J. *The Index of Leading Cultural Indicators*. Washington, DC: The Heritage Foundation, 1993.

Bible Quizzing Fellowship. "Bible Quiz Fellowship - A Fellowship of Youth Ministries," http://www.biblequizfellowship.org.

Brown, Scott. "Children in the Meeting of the Ephesian Church" 2004, Vision Forum Ministries,

http://www.visionforumministries.org/issues/uniting_church_a
nd_family/children_in_the_meeting_of_the.aspx
Calvin, John. "Aphorisms." In *Institutes of The Christian Religion*.
Translated by Hevry Beveridge. Grand Rapids, MI: Eerdmans
Publishing, 1997.
Charlotte Thomson Iserbyt. "The Deliberate Dumbing Down of
America," 2000. Charlotte Thomson Iserbyt.
http://www.delberatedumbindown.com.
Christenson, Larry. *The Christian Family*. Minneapolis, MN:
Bethany Fellowship, 1970.
Christian Research Association. "Implication of the Study of
Youth Spirituality," September, 2006.
http://www.cra.org.au/pages/000000269.cgi.
Clarke, Adam. "Deuteronomy." In *Adam Clark's Commentary On
The Bible*.
Colson, Charles, and Ellen Santilli Vaughn. *Against The Night:
Living in The New Dark Ages*. Grand Rapids, Michigan:
Zondervan, 1999.
Dauphinais, Brandon. "The Age-Integrated Church," 2002. B.
Dauphinais. http://www.utmost-
way.com/theageintegratedchurcharticle.htm.
David Guzik's Commentary. "Ephesians," StudyLight.org.
http://www.studylight.org/com/guz/view.
David Martyn Lloyd-Jones. "Nurture and Admonition." *Free
Grace Broadcaster* 208 (Summer 2008).
DeVries Mark, "Youth Ministry 101" 2007, Youth Ministry.Com,
www.youthministry.com/?q=node/5499
Duea, David. "Child and Family Guidance Center," 2008.
http://www.cfgpc.org/impact.htm.
Edwards Jonathan, "Works of Jonathan Edwards Volume Two:
Examining the Lord's Day"
http://www.ccel.org/ccel/edwards/works2.vi.v.v.html?highlight
=church,instructing,children#highlight
Elwell, Walter A. *Evangelical Dictionary of Theology*. Grand Rapids,

MI: Baker Books, 1984.

Evans, Craig A. *The New International Biblical Commentary - Luke*. Peabody, Ma: Hendrickson Publishers, 1998.

First Family Church. "Welcome To First Family Church," October, 2008. First Family Church. http://www.ffc.org.

Fox, J. Mark. *Family Integrated Church*. Camirillo, California: Salem Communications, 2006.

Fugate, J. Richard. *What The Bible Says About Child Training*, Second ed. Apache Junction, Arizona: Foundation For Biblical Research, 1999.

Geisler, Norman. *Systematic Theology Volume Two: God and Creation*. Minneapolis, Minnesota: Bethany House, 2005.

GFBC. "Alliance for Church & Family Reformation," September, 2008. GFBC. http://www.gracefamilybaptist.net.

Gill, John. "Acts." In *The New John Gill's Exposition of The Entire Bible*. Paris AR: The Baptist Standard Bearer, 1999.

Hampton James, Mark Hayse, "A Different View of Family Ministry" 2009, Youth Specialties, http://www.youthspecialties.com/freeresources/articles/family/different_view.php

Hartley, John E. *The New International Biblical Commentary - Genesis*. Peabody, Ma: Hendrickson Publishers, 2000.

Healy, Anthony E. "Questioning the Age-Segregated Church," September, 2003. http://www.alban.org/conversation.aspx?id=2416.

Hodge, Charles. *Systematic Theology Volume III*, Fourth ed. Peabody, MA: Hendrickson Publishers, 2008.

"Homeschooling Research," October, 2008. http://www.hslda.org/research/faq.asp.

John, Angell James. "Principle Obstacles in Bringing Up Children for Christ." *Free Grace Broadcaster* 208 (Summer 2008).

Katz, Lilian. "The Benefits of the Mix," November, 1998. Child Care Information Exchange. http://www.childcareexchange.com.

Klick, Jeffrey A. *Bumper Car Theology*. Morrisville, North Carolina: Lulu Publishing, 2006.

Lewis, C. S. *The Abolition of Man*. San Francisco, CA: Harper Collins Publishers, 1944.

Luther - The large catechism the Fourth Commandment. http://www.ccel.org/ccel/luther/large_cat/files/large_catechism06.htm

Luther – Table Talk http://www.ccel.org/ccel/luther/tabletalk.v.xvii.html?highlight= children,teaching#highlight

Luther - Treatise on Good Works http://www.ccel.org/ccel/luther/good_works.vii.html?highlight =school#highlight

McNeal, Reggie. *The Present Future*. San Francisco, California: Bass, Jossey, 2003.

Melton, Alan. "Quality Time" 2007, The Association for the Restoration of Church and Home, http://www.restorechurchandhome.org/index.php?option=com _content&task=view&id=28&Itemid=32

Michel, Jarrod. 2008 Household Approach to Ministry; Rebuilding the Foundations of Family, Faith and Ministry. Master's thesis, Denver Seminary

Ministry.com. "YouthMinistry.com - One Place, Infinite Ideas," http://www.youthministry.com.

Nair, Ken. *Discovering the Mind of a Woman*. Nashville, Tennessee: Thomas Nelson, 1995.

National Youth Workers Convention. http://www.nywc.com. "New Marriage and Divorce Statistics Released," M ARCH. Association for The Restoration of Church and Home. http://www.restorechurchandhome.org.

Orthodox Presbyterian Church. "Westminster Confession of Faith," http://www.opc.org/wcf.html.

Pearl, Michael. *To Train Up a Child*. Pleasantville, Tennessee: Michael Pearl Publishing, 1994.

Phillips, Doug. Vision Forum Ministries.
http://www.visionforumministries.org.
Phillips, Doug Esq., "Our Church Youth Group" 2002, Vision
Forum Ministries,
http://www.visionforumministries.org/issues/uniting_church_a
nd_family/our_church_youth_group.aspx
Pinkney, T. C. Remarks to the Southern Baptist Convention
Executive Committee. Nashville, Tennessee, 2001.
Pray 4 Revival Youth Ministries, N/A. http://www.injesus.com.
Ray, Brian D. Ray Ph.D. "Home Educated and Now Adults:
Their Community and Civic Involvement, Views About
Homeschooling, and Other Traits," 2008. National Home
Education Research Institute. http://www.nheri.org/Home-
Educated-and-Now-Adults.html.
Ryle, J. C. "Primary Obligation of Parents." *Free Grace Broadcaster*
208 (Summer 2008).
Schlect, Chris. "A Critique of Youth Ministries,"
http://www.soulcare.org/education/youth.
Schuchmann, Linda. "Role modeling for Children," 2008. Boys
Town.
http://www.parenting.org/guidance/rolemodelingforchildren.as
p.
Schaeffer, Francis A. *The Church At The End of The 20th Century.*
Downers Grove, Il: Varsity Press, Inter, 1972
Sheldon and Eleanor Glueck. *Unraveling Juvenile Delinquency.*
Cambridge, MS: Harvard University Press, 1950.
Silberman, John. Crisis in The Classroom: The Remaking of
American Education. New York, NY: Random House, 1970.
"Sparking Revival in Tomorrow's Church Leaders," April 9,
2008. http://www.gospel.com.
Syndicate PayScale Data. "Salary Survey Report for Job: Youth
Pastor," 9/4/2008.
http://www.payscale.com/research/US/Job=Youth_Pastor.

The Alban Institute. 2008.
http://www.alban.org/conversation.aspx?id=2416.
The Association for the Restoration of Church and Home.
"ARCH," September, 2008.
http://www.restorechurchandhome.org.
"The Call DC," April 11, 2008. http://www.thecall.com.
The New International Biblical Commentary. Peabody, Ma:
Hendrickson Publishers, 2000.
The Source For Youth Ministry. "Sick and Twisted Games,"
http://www.thesource4ym.com/games/sick.asp.
Today, Christian. "Methodist Youth Conference Calls for Prayer
of Revival," Wednesday, June 28, 2006. Christian Today.
http://www.christiantoday.com/article/myc.call.for.prayer.for.re
vival/6763.htm.
United States Government. "Morbidity and Mortality Weekly
Report," June 6, 2008. Surveillance Summaries.
http://www.cdc.gov/mmwr.
Vine, W. E. *An Expository Dictionary of New Testament Words.* Old
Tappan, NJ: Fleming H. Revell, 1966.
Vision Forum Ministries, September, 2008. The National
Centering for Family-integrated Churches.
http://www.visionforumministries.org.
Wells, David F. *God in The Wasteland; The Reality of Truth in a
World of Fading Dreams.* Grand Rapids, MI: Eerdmans, 1994.
Wells, David F. *No Place for Truth, Or Whatever Happened to
Evangelical Theology?* Grand Rapids, MI: Eerdmans Publishing,
1993.
Williams, J. Rodman. *Renewal Theology - The Church, The Kingdom,
and Last Things.* Grand Rapids, MI: Zondervan Publishing House,
1992.

Made in the USA
Charleston, SC
31 July 2014